NORTHUMBERLAND WALKS FOR MOTORISTS

Warne Gerrard Guides for Walkers

NORTHUMBERLAND

WALKS FOR MOTORISTS

Compiled by members of the Ramblers' Association, Northern Area

Sketch maps by C. G. Edwards and D. L. Indge

FREDERICK WARNE

FREDERICK WARNE
Penguin Books Ltd, Harmondsworth, Middlesex, England
Viking Penguin Inc., 40 West 23rd Street, New York, New York 10010, U.S.A.
Penguin Books Australia Ltd, Ringwood, Victoria, Australia
Penguin Books Canada Limited, 2801 John Street, Markham, Ontario, Canada L3R 1B4
Penguin Books (N.Z.) Ltd, 182–190 Wairau Road, Auckland 10, New Zealand

First published 1981
Reprinted with revisions 1982
Second edition 1986

The photograph on the front cover shows the Park Burn on Plenmeller Common, south of Haltwhistle, and was taken by I. M. H. Fletcher.

Publishers' Note

While every care has been taken in the compilation of this book, the publishers cannot accept responsibility for any inaccuracies. But things change: paths are sometimes diverted; concrete bridges replace wooden ones; stiles disappear. Please inform the publishers if you discover anything like this on your way.

The length of each walk in this book is given in miles and kilometres, but within the text Imperial measurements are quoted. It is useful to bear the following approximations in mind: 5 miles = 8 kilometres, ½ mile = 805 metres, 1 metre = 39.4 inches.

Made and printed in Great Britain by
Cox & Wyman, Reading

Contents

To the memory of Frank Gillan, who
made a considerable contribution towards
the production of this book and a lifetime's
contribution to the work of the Ramblers'
Association, Northern Area

Introduction

Perhaps the charm of much of Northumberland is its remoteness and absence of crowds, its appeal being in inverse proportion to the numbers who enjoy it. There are nevertheless popular and overburdened 'honey-pots' such as Hadrian's Wall and parts of the coast, and these have been avoided for the purpose of this book – it being assumed that the walker enjoys space and quiet. There are also large expanses which are unsuitable for various reasons. Man-made and closely planted forest, the biggest in Europe, overspreads much of the National Park. Between the A68 in upper Redesdale and the valley of the Coquet, the Army has a vast firing range to which there is no access for most of the year. The remoter parts of the Cheviots are so far from roads that they can be reached only by strenuous walkers.

In so large a county there is much scenic variety. The uplands, Cheviots and North Pennines, rising to well over 2,000 feet, are massed to the west and are bisected by the Tyne Gap. The south-east is a broad plain. Between them the volcanic intrusion of the Great Whin Sill thrusts up across the county from the north-east coast, where it forms cliffs, many inland facing and known locally as 'heughs'; to the west where the scarp slopes face north and have provided the Romans with a natural line of defence for their wall.

The Cheviots and Pennines are rounded with relatively little rock outcrop and grow rough tussocky grass, heather and bracken. There are peat 'hags' and bogs but few topographical dangers. The valleys and lowlands outside the industrial south-east are pastoral and agricultural. The coast has incomparable sandy beaches.

Northumberland's climate is not the mildest nor driest and its public footpaths are frequently undefined and over rough terrain. Intending walkers should equip themselves with strong boots, waterproofs and woollens and carry rucksacks for food, drink and spare clothing. The life of the countryside should be respected and care taken to close gates, avoid alarming or disturbing animals or causing any kind of damage to property.

Northumberland is beautiful. Please help to keep it so.

The OS sheet number at the head of each walk refers to the Ordnance Survey 1:50,000 series of maps. The sketch maps herein should be sufficient, but a full map undoubtedly adds interest.

NORTHUMBERLAND

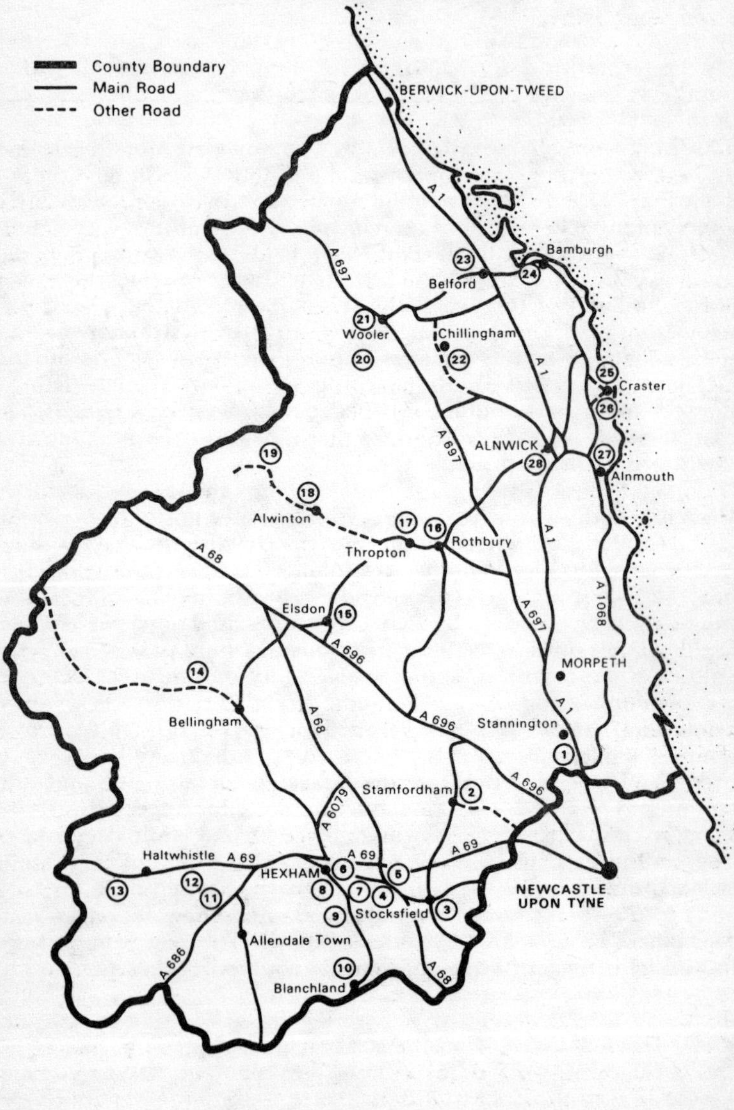

Numbers denote approximate location of walk.

Walk 1 Stannington and Bellasis

6 miles (9.5 km)

OS sheet 88, grid ref 213789

This walk would be suitable for a fine summer evening in late May or June when there is plenty of daylight and the rush of the day is over. Part of it is briefly along the A1 and another road which carries a fair amount of traffic, but there is plenty of roadside verge for safe walking. It is an easy, flat walk through fields, woods and quiet estate roads for most of its length, on a route with recent official diversions of rights of way as at present shown on the Ordnance Survey map. All footpaths with their diversions are very clearly way-marked and there should be no difficulty in finding the correct route.

There are several possible parking areas. These are mentioned in the text and shown on the map. The route is described from the by-road west of the A1, just south of Stannington.

Walk south away from Stannington. Pass the end of the private road to Vale and cross the road bridge over the river Blyth. There is ample parking space on a continuation, parallel to the A1, of the run-in from near Blagdon Hall and alongside the grounds. At the north end of this parking space a public footpath sign indicates the direction of Ponteland. It is a surfaced estate road and a right of way for pedestrians. Follow it to the line of cottages at New Kennels and along the front of these as directed by another sign and a yellow arrow. The farm with the tall silos further off on the left is the Home Farm of the Blagdon estate.

At the corner shortly before that leave the road and go under the paling (not through the gate on the right) and along the track between the woodland and the wire fence. At the end of the field the path goes into the woods via a gap. It is a pleasant grass track under tall pine and oak and smaller spruce plantings. Cross an estate road and continue, as indicated by the sign, through the woods. At the end of the trees there is a stile beside a gate. Go into the field and turn immediately left along the edge of it to a wicket gate leading out on to an estate road. Turn right along this towards a farm and follow the road round over a little stream. The farm over on the right now is Bog House. Continue on the straight road due south, passing the end of the turning off to Bog House. Further south O.S. maps show a right of way to the east of this lane but this has been transferred to the lane. At the time of writing there is open cast coal mining on

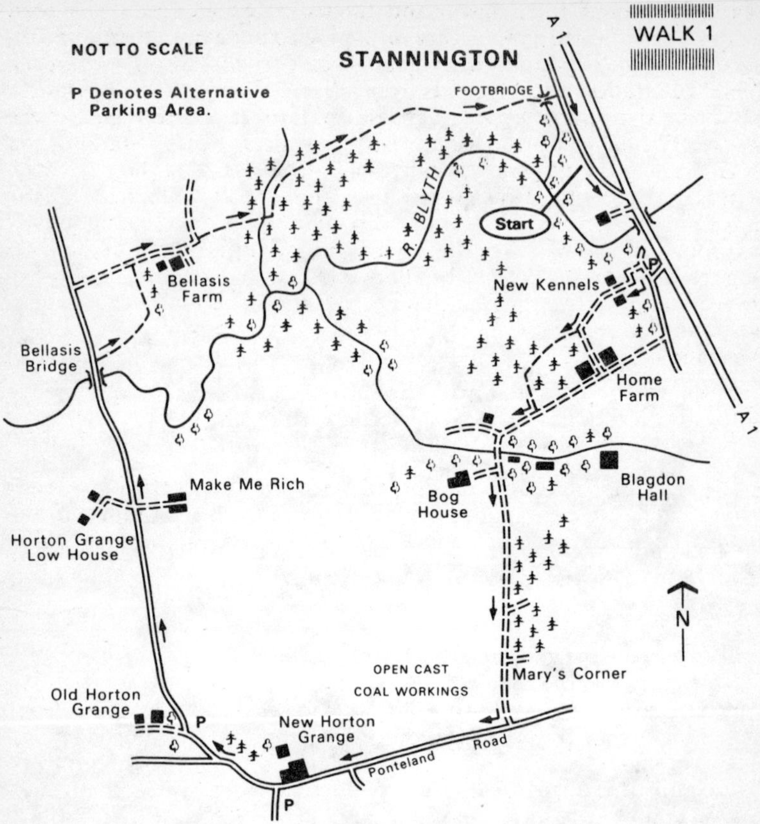

a small site to the west. Pass cross-tracks at Mary's Corner and continue to the Ponteland road.

Turn right and walk along the grass verge for almost a mile to New Horton Grange. Woodland shown on the O.S. map has been felled for the open-cast coal mining. Go past the handsome Horton Grange and the cottages to the Make-me-rich and Bellasis road on the right. Now walk north on this very quiet road. There is a useful parking space at the side of this road about a hundred yards from the corner. Further on a side road goes off to Old Horton Grange. Continue on the Bellasis road. Cross straight over where side drives lead off to Make-me-rich and Horton Grange Low House.

Just over the hump-backed Bellasis bridge over the river Blyth is a stile and a footpath sign pointing to Stannington. Follow the path along the left side of the wire fence. This is the line of the original right of way but there is a diversion at the far end of the field. Turn left as indicated by the signs and go up to the farm road to Bellasis.

Walk right along to the farm and then straight on where the road swings right and through a gate or over the stile where the footpath-sign points to Stannington. A good broad track leads into Church Wood plantation and descends over a burn, then turns immediately left as the sign indicates, through the trees to the north edge, where it veers right and continues to a stile out into a field. Stannington church tower is visible now. Walk along the left edge of the field. The next stile has been placed a few feet from the corner to avoid the muddy area. Continue in the same direction to the next diversion part way along the field, where there are further footpath signs and a little stagger in the fence. Bear right and walk diagonally across to a line of three hawthorn trees and another angle of fence, about 40 yd from the woodland on the right. There is an isolated gatepost here. Continue from the angle alongside the fence to the next stile. There may be a lot of bullocks in this field. They may galumph about in a giddy fashion and be very interested in, but hopefully not hostile to, ramblers. The stile again avoids the churned-up 'clarts' in the field corner.

Climb over into the plantation and turn right and then down left over a rather slippery plank bridge over a deep burn hidden in tall plants. The path comes out shortly on to the road just south of Stannington, where the walk began.

Walk 2 Stamfordham and Eachwick

6 miles (9.5 km)

OS sheet 88, grid ref 078721

This walk begins from the village of Stamfordham which is about 14 miles north-west of Newcastle. It is an easy walk over fields and along riversides.

Stamfordham has a wide green with stone terraced houses facing each other across it and, free-standing between them, a market cross, an old lock-up and the village local. At the western end is the 13th-century Church of St Mary, and the vicarage; at the eastern end are the schools.

Walk to the east end of the green then right on the B6309 and cross over to take the lane between the council houses and the new school past a group of lock-up garages. At the end of the lane is a field gate with a stile to the left. Go along the top of the field and through the gate in the staggered field boundary ahead and keeping in the same direction, continue with the hedge now on the right. Below Chapel Farm and through the gate the path turns half right and goes down to the far south-east corner to Nettley Bank above the infant Pont. The exit to Nettley Bank is at the extreme end of the barbed-wire fence where there is a narrow gap over the fence.

Follow the bank along to a wide metal gate and then on to a new stile to the right of High Farm. Turn right and walk down past Four Winds and Heugh Mill to the main road. Turn right again and cross the Pont by the road bridge. Just on the other side there is a stile in the wall on the left and a good clear track, the Captain's Walk, along the bankside by the grounds of Cheeseburn Grange. The Grange is not visible from here but there are many fine trees: beech, pine, yew, oak, larch, lime and horse-chestnut.

Where the grounds open out beyond the walled garden there is a field on the right. Keep to the path along the outside edge of this until a broken stile leads over to a short lonnen on the right. Go on in the same direction along this and through a wicket gate into a field ahead.

Now turn right and away from the river Pont and walk down the edge of the field with trees behind a wall on the right. There is a boggy section at the south end of this field and the stile is on the far side in the corner, so some care is needed.

Eachwick Red House, the next landmark to aim to, is now visible

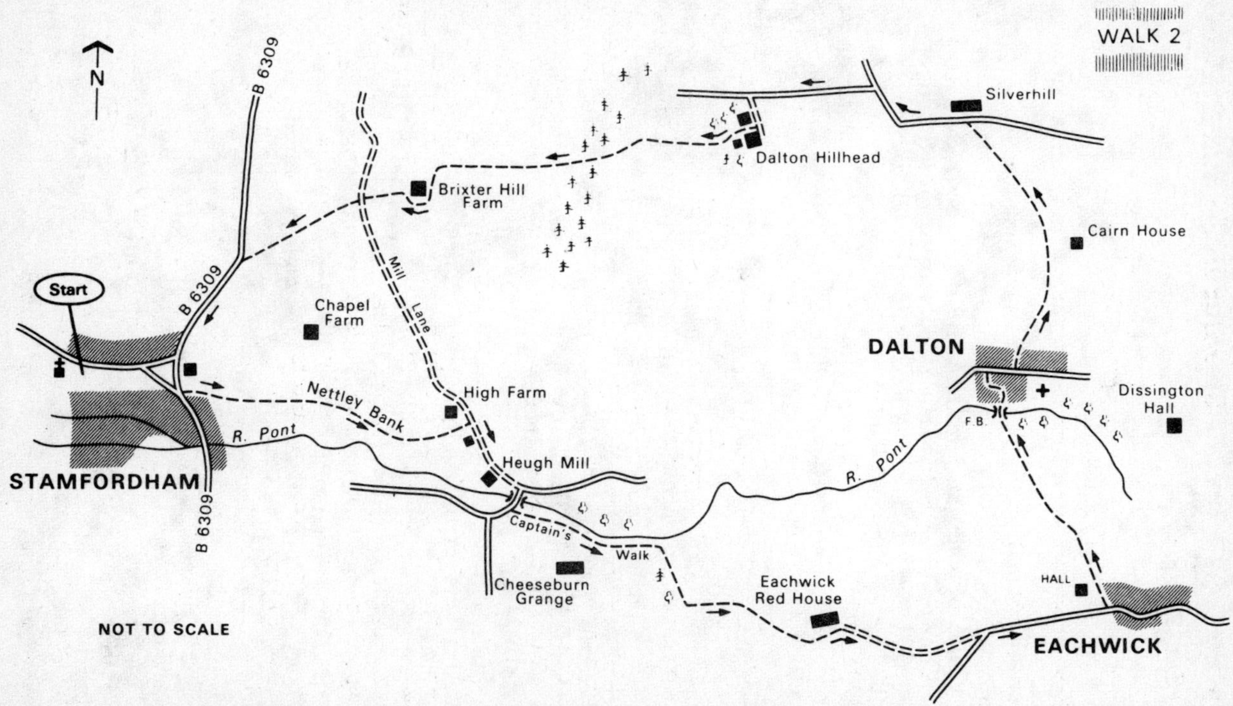
WALK 2
N
Start
STAMFORDHAM
B 6309
B 6309
B 6309
Chapel Farm
Mill Lane
Nettley Bank
R. Pont
High Farm
Heugh Mill
Brixter Hill Farm
Dalton Hillhead
Silverhill
Cairn House
DALTON
F.B.
Dissington Hall
R. Pont
Captain's Walk
Cheeseburn Grange
Eachwick Red House
HALL
EACHWICK
NOT TO SCALE

to the east. Over the stile turn left and walk along the field edge to a lane and along to the front of the house. Follow the track as it curves round the front of the house towards the corrugated iron barn. Through the wide double gates turn sharp right on to another surfaced lane and over the cattle grid bear left along the minor road to Eachwick Hall. Notice the stone birds on the parapet here.

The right of way leaves the road immediately beyond the entrance gates to Eachwick Hall and goes along what seems to be the drive to the shuttered house next to it. At the back of the garden a stile leads out into a field. Walk north beside the wall of Eachwick Hall grounds and follow them left for a short distance at the end; then north-west again along the field boundary. At the end of the field go through the wide gate ahead, not the wicket on the left. Continue in the same direction with the field boundary on the left. Out of sight on the right, because it is flowing in a deep cleugh, is the river Pont and visible beyond it is Dissington Hall.

At the north end a stile leads into a copse surrounding a disused quarry and the path descends steeply via old steps to a county footbridge over the Pont. Cross to the ruined Dalton Mill and follow the path round two sides of it to a track behind it. Walk left a few yards; then right up a few stone steps with a hand rail, to a lonnen beside a brick bungalow; then out on to the road via a kissing gate.

This is Dalton. Turn right and walk a short distance towards the church, then turn left between the old school building and the cottages. Pass the line of garages and cross a stile beside a wide gate. The footpath is narrow between a berberis hedge and a wire fence bordering a paddock. It emerges in a slightly staggered line into a field beyond. Walk diagonally right across here to the north-east corner passing an old iron boiler top which provides a landmark. Cairn House, with what appears to be a weaving gallery on the near side, is one field away on the right. There is a wide gate at the top. Continue along the right-hand sides of the fields to Silverhill, where there is a stile out on to the road.

Turn left and walk on the road for about half-a-mile to Dalton Hillhead, en route following the signpost direction towards 'Heugh 1½, Stamfordham 2½'. Turn left off the road at Dalton Hillhead and then right past the end of the farm through a narrow gap between wooden buildings and a little stone barn. Go straight on through the trees towards a wide gate but not through it. Over to the left is a large pond surrounded by a swampy area. The right of way goes down towards this and crosses into it at the corner. In very wet conditions turn round the end of the fence and cross into the wet area as soon as practicable. With the fence alongside continue west.

Through a gate at the end of this enclosure cut across the corner to the stile about 75 yd to the left. Do not use the stile in the corner, although both lead into the plantation. Go through the trees by a narrow ride to a forest track on the far side and cross this, bearing left a little to a stile partially hidden behind a gorse bush and leading into the corner of a field. Walk due west with the field boundary on the right. At the far end of the second field the route goes left towards Brixter Hill Farm and then round the south side of it and back via a gate to the same general line again, using the farm road out on to Mill Lane.

Cross this diagonally left and then via the wooden field gate keep to the right-hand side of the following fields in a direct line south-west to a bend in the road, which leads down left, in under a quarter-mile, to Stamfordham.

Walk 3 — Stockfield, High Mickley and Broomleyhope Wood

8 miles (13 km)

OS sheets 87 & 88, grid ref 054612

The walk begins from the by-road off the main A695 opposite Stocksfield Station. It is a field and woodland walk on fairly easy terrain but requiring careful navigation and map reading.

Walk east on the pavement along the main road from the station past the modern estate to Merryshield Terrace, a row of stone cottages facing west, and turn left immediately beyond them on a footpath signposted to Eltringham and Ovingham. This path joins a wide gravel track a few yards beyond the end of the cottages. Continue on this past Merryshield Farm and through a small gate to the left of the field gate.

The track forks ahead. Ignore the right branch which leads to Merryshield Common and take the other past a wide metal gate. Keep to the right of the fence, following the main track into the woods. This becomes rougher and muddier, but work is under way to improve it. Keep in the same general direction ignoring a branch to the left and continue through the broom, silver birch and elms, past a tiny pond, where the woods give way to rolling grassland, the reclaimed humps of old spoil heaps. Aim to the right of a copse of silver birch passing a distinct cleft in the small hills to the right and ascending the lower slope of Bullion Hills at the foot of a miniature sandy scarp. Go over the rise and follow a line of hawthorn trees to a descending fence on the near side of two fields. The right of way is along the north, i.e. left, side of the boundary between these fields. It is necessary to climb the paling in the descending fence. Continue due east to a gate leading into a grassy lane and turn right along this for a few yards, then left over a stile beside a wide gate.

Eltringham House is ahead. Go through the wide gate to the right of the house and garden and out on to the corner of a road via a short lane. Turn left and downhill past old arched buildings, the remnants of past industry, to the crossroads below. Take the right-hand narrow road curving uphill past the bungalow, Oakwood, and on to where the surface becomes softer, more of a grit track. Towards the end of a line of trees on the right and just as the houses of Prudhoe come into view a path leads off via a stile through the long woodland, curving gradually uphill. Where it diverges bear slightly left keeping nearer

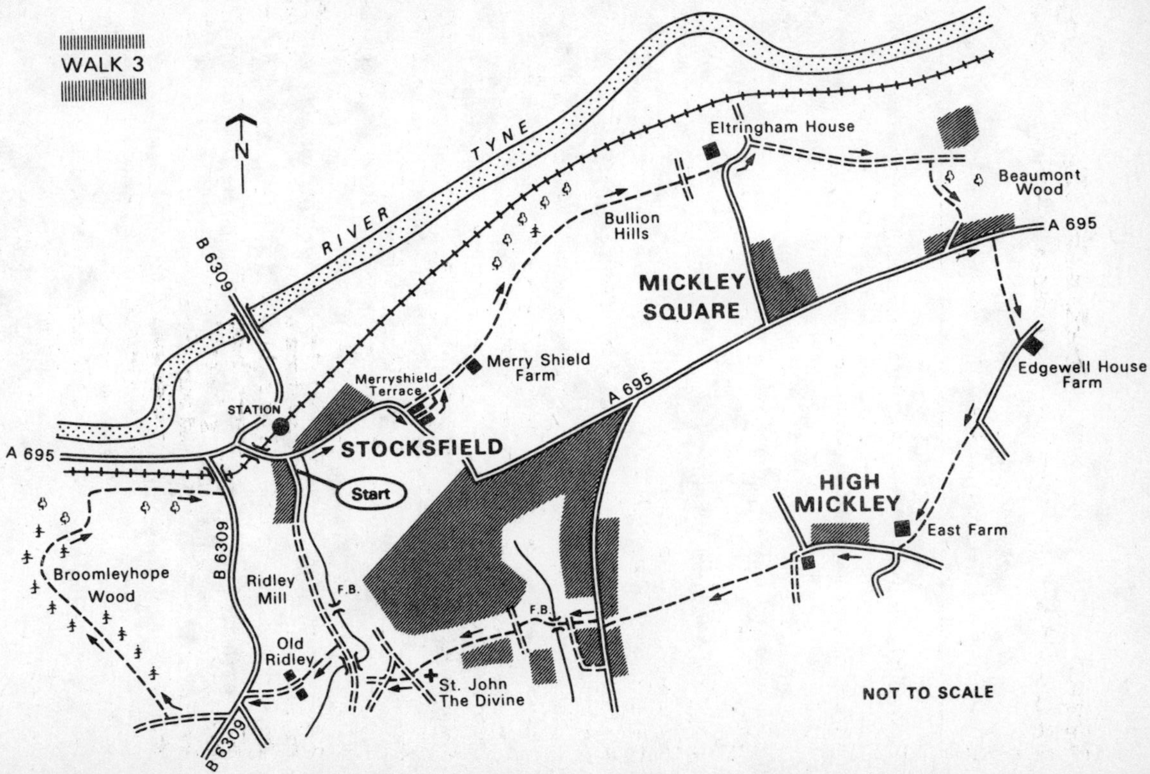
WALK 3
N
RIVER TYNE
B 6309
STATION
A 695
STOCKSFIELD
Start
Merryshield Terrace
Merry Shield Farm
Bullion Hills
Eltringham House
Beaumont Wood
A 695
MICKLEY SQUARE
A 695
Edgewell House Farm
HIGH MICKLEY
East Farm
Broomleyhope Wood
B 6309
Ridley Mill
F.B.
Old Ridley
St. John The Divine
F.B.
B 6309
NOT TO SCALE

to the left side of the woods but maintaining the same general direction uphill. Cross over at cross-tracks and continue up until the path veers left below a hut and fence. Soon it comes out on to Eltringham road. Turn right and up to the main road at Prudhoe.

This is the A695 again. Turn left along Beaumont Terrace almost to the east end of it and cross to a footpath sign pointing up the fields on the opposite side of the main road. Climb the stile to the left of the gate and go directly uphill by the wire fence, round the angle and up to the good stile.

Keep in the same direction in the next field and up to the road in front of Edgewell House Farm, with its old 'gin gang', where horse power in its literal sense was used for grinding the corn.

Turn right on this road and walk west to the first sharp bend where a public footpath sign points straight on. Climb the stile beside the wide gate and follow the tracks along the top of the fields. There are fine views over the Tyne valley from here and on clear days the Cheviots, Hedgehope and the Simonsides are visible on the northern skyline. Continue along the field edges to the left side of East Farm and a wicket gate in the corner. Through this cross by the left of a few trees to a wide field gate then diagonally left over a long narrow pasture to a gate out on to the farm lane.

Go left and almost immediately out on to the road, then right for a few yards to the corner of the Hedley road. Bear right a little and slightly downhill to the hamlet of High Mickley. Continue to the west edge of the hamlet but do not follow the road downhill. Keeping at the same level follow the wide track to the corner where there are three footpath signs together. To avoid recent ploughing, turn left for a few yards, then through the gate into the field on the right. Follow the double field track which runs alongside a hedge, walking west in a straight line through the fields, and then downhill into the steep gorse-grown pasture where the land dips into the valley of the Stocksfield Burn. The right of way is to the right of a line of hawthorn trees descending to the lower end of the pasture. It continues to the New Ridley road via a narrow gap between gardens.

Turn right for about 50 yd, cross to a footpath sign and follow this between, then alongside gardens and across an estate road down to a footbridge over a little burn. Follow the path right and then left along the perimeter of a new house and its garden, and continue until it emerges on to a tree-lined road. Turn right for a yard or so and cross to an entry to another path down the edges of more gardens. This path comes out beside the Church of St John the Divine. Cross slightly left and through another entry to a small park and follow the path across to the far side to a wicket out on to the corner of a road. Go straight ahead past the front of a row of terraced cottages keeping to the upper road at the Y junction and to the right of the 'Painshawfield Road' sign. At the end of the cul-de-sac descend the steps at Windward Cottage to the Ridley Mill road below. Turn right and cross the road bridge over the Stocksfield Burn.

To return directly to base from here, continue to follow the Stocksfield Burn downstream past Ridley Mill and on through the housing estate to the road toward Stocksfield Station.

For the longer walk to Broomleyhope Wood turn left along the rather muddy lane up through the hamlet of Old Ridley and out on to the Hindley road. Cross to the left and turn almost immediately right up a lane. Follow this to a junction where a notice 'Footpath only, no horse riding' indicates the track curving right off the lane and under the tall pines. Keep to this well-defined woodland path for about half a mile, the fields to the east within fairly close proximity all the way, to a distinct crossing of tracks where directions are indicated by small purple squares with arrows. Turn sharp right here on a narrower path towards a gate into a field but do *not* go through. The path keeps to the near side of the fence and crosses an expanse of cleared forest, rough grass growing up round the bases of the sawn-off trunks. The deep little cleugh to the left is the Smithy Burn. Turn left downhill beside the new barbed wire fence and cross by the stile into the long sloping pasture. Drop down to the woodland below and turn right along the little ridge to where the trees peter out into a long pasture beside the railway cutting. Continue to the eastern corner where there is a kissing gate out on to the Hindley road and a footpath sign pointing back to Broomley.

Turn left and cross the railway bridge to the main road, the A695, and return to Stocksfield Station.

Walk 4 Corbridge, Dipton Wood and Slaley

10½ miles (17 km)

OS sheet 87, grid ref 990635 (Corbridge station)

This is a long walk through the fields and woods on the south side of Corbridge. It can be shortened, if required, by using minor roads—but do not try to walk the path between Marley Cote Walls and West Woodfoot farms as there is almost impassable mud and sludge near East Woodfoot. There are parking spaces near Corbridge station and a pull-in on the A6080 a few yards west of the walk.

From Corbridge station cross the road-bridge or the foot-bridge over the railway to the south side and use the steps at the angle of the road to climb diagonally up through a recently felled copse known as 'The Scroggs'. From the kissing gate follow up the field edges and cross the A6080 using the stiles, then straight on and over Ladycutter's Lane and uphill through a narrow copse to a stile on to a path beside a hedge.

Turn right along the minor road from Mount Pleasant and continue to the T junction. Turn right again and walk as far as the drive between Fell Top and Temperley Grange. Turn left along this and follow the field edges beside the wall to the stone stile in the corner out on to the road which skirts Dipton Wood. This is one of the possible points for shortening the walk. (See sketch map.) For the longer walk follow the road left downhill to a gate just past the wall enclosing the east edge of the plantation, then turn right along the wide track under tall trees. The handsome Dipton House is on the bankside over to the left.

Keep alongside the rather broken wall, ignoring any tracks off to the left, and follow the yellow way-markers down to cross the Dipton Burn by a single plank bridge. Ascend the far bank on the narrow path towards the edge of the wood and the gorse bushes. In summer this path is crawling with ants so picnicking is not advised!

At the broad rough track turn left between walls and climb the ladder stile near Todburn Steel Farm. A few yards to the right is another stile into a field. Over this, turn left alongside a narrow plantation and through another gate a little to the right beyond that. Follow the western perimeter in the next field and come out on to the North Road via a stone stile in the corner. This road provides another route for shortening the walk if required. For the full walk cross straight over to a stone stile. North Wood Plantation shown to the

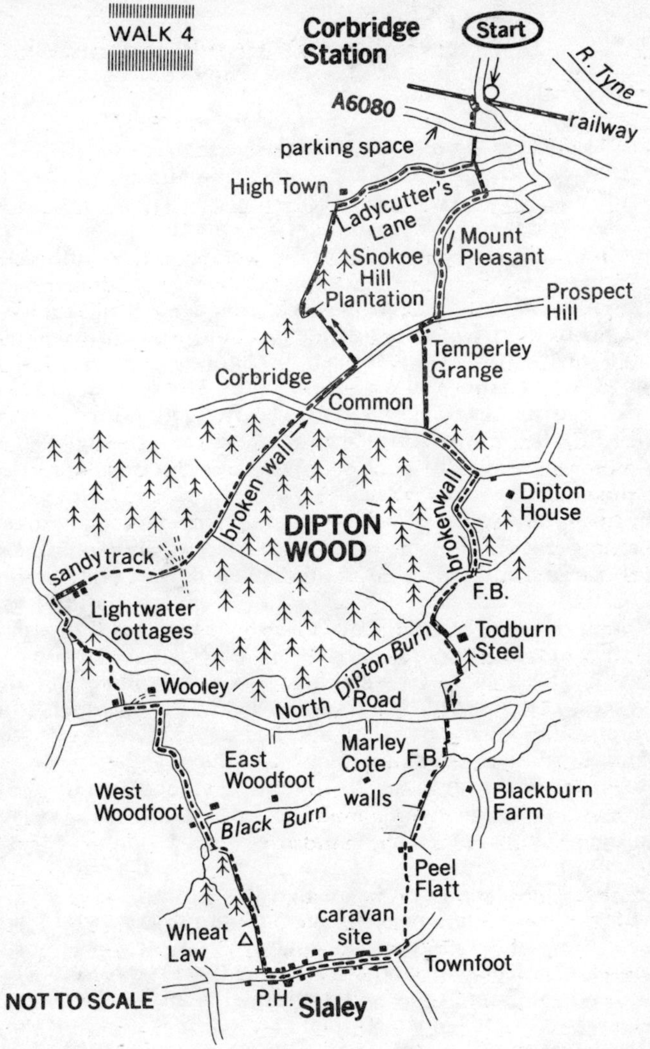

WALK 4
Corbridge Station
Start
R. Tyne
A6080
railway
parking space
High Town
Ladycutter's Lane
Mount Pleasant
Snokoe Hill Plantation
Prospect Hill
Temperley Grange
Corbridge Common
broken wall
DIPTON WOOD
brokenwall
Dipton House
sandy track
F.B.
Lightwater cottages
Todburn Steel
North Dipton Burn
Wooley
North Road
Marley Cote
East Woodfoot
F.B.
West Woodfoot
walls
Blackburn Farm
Black Burn
Peel Flatt
caravan site
Wheat Law
Townfoot
NOT TO SCALE
P.H.
Slaley

right on OS maps was felled a few years ago.

Continue down the field edge with the fence right then cross the stile and continue south with the fence left. Cross the Black Burn by the double plank footbridge and follow the fence roughly south-west to a stone stile which brings you to the other side of the field boundary. Now walk with a wall, then a fence, on the right to the farm road at Peel Flatt. Pass the farmhouse and go through the field gate and slightly downhill. Then, looking for the new tall ladder stiles ahead, walk through the fields south to a copse to the left of the caravan site at Slaley Townfoot. A low stone stile leads out on to the road. Walk west through the village of Slaley as far as the church. The Fox and Hounds in the centre of Slaley is now open at lunchtime and serves bar meals.

The Church of St Mary the Virgin, which is the return point for the walk, dates from 1832 when it replaced a much older one whose history dated back to the thirteenth century. Follow the track to the right of the church north past Wheat Law, the grassy dome on the left, and descend alongside a plantation to the little valley of the Black Burn which flows from a large pond. The track rises slightly and continues to a surfaced road at West Woodfoot. Keep to the road north-north-west to the North Road at Wooley.

Between the wars Wooley was a sanatorium for tuberculosis sufferers; then for a time it served as a convalescent home. Now it has been sold and the dilapidated wards pulled down. The right of way through the grounds has been diverted a few yards to the west. Walk left along the road past the smart new entrance gates to a pair of stiles leading to a coniferous plantation. The path keeps to the east of the wood for a short distance then crosses diagonally left and follows the west side through the trees down to a fence which runs along the top of the bank above the Dipton Burn. Turn left over the stile here and, keeping the bank-top fence fairly close alongside on the right, pick your way through the slightly tangled woodland until the path emerges into the open. Still with the fence alongside, look for the stile in the far north-eastern corner; it is way-marked.

Go into Dipton Wood edge and follow the pine-needle path which keeps to a little spur down to the road in the Dipton Burn valley. Continue north on the road over the burn and up to the second gate on the right and the forest road to Lightwater Cottages. Shortly before these are reached a sandy track leaves the road and goes straight on up through the trees and occasional clumps of heather to the taller, more closely planted, part of the wood. Where the track joins another forest track bear left a little and walk in a fairly straight line north-easterly. The track is quite broad and clear except where forestry clearing has churned up the ground and hidden the exact line but in wet weather places are very muddy. An old broken wall which can be glimpsed at intervals on the right provides a useful guide to those in doubt or without a compass. Eventually the track emerges on to the road at Corbridge Common.

Cross over and follow the minor road towards Temperley Grange and Prospect Hill. After about a quarter-mile a good track leads off left alongside fields to Snokoe Hill Plantation. Go into the wood and turn left downhill, keeping near the edge. The beginning of the forest track is rough and uneven but it soon improves. At the corner turn right and keep to the good clear track which descends to the west side and turns right again down the inside edge of this fine old mixed plantation—much of it, alas, now felled. At the lowest corner, just above High Town Farm, turn right and follow Ladycutter's Lane to the point where it was crossed at the beginning of the walk. Retrace the first section back to base.

Walk 5 — Corbridge, Aydon Castle and Thornbrough

5 miles (8 km)

OS sheet 87, grid ref 988644

This is an easy walk through fields and woodland on the north side of Corbridge. There is some unavoidable road walking, mainly on very quiet minor roads. Short stretches at the beginning and end, along busier roads, have good wide pavements in each case.

There is parking space in the market place and the walk is described from here.

Leave the market place between the pele tower in the church grounds and the Methodist chapel. The old market cross beside the pele tower entrance stood in the market place for 600 years, then was re-erected on its present site in 1975. The cut leads through to Hill Street just opposite the post office. Turn right, then left at the T-junction, and continue up Princes Street. Keep on this road, the B6321, on the left-hand pavement, passing the old vicarage, the new Glebelands housing estate, St Helen's Lane, and the police station. At Riversdale, a large brick-built house with stone gate posts, turn left and then almost immediately right into a long cul-de-sac which tapers off to a bridleway, signposted to 'Aydon Dene, 1; Aydon Castle 2'.

Continue north to the new A69, the Corbridge and Hexham by-pass. Here the bridleway has been diverted east to a bridge carrying the B6321 over the busy motor road. Cross by the bridge and return to the original line of the route via the diversion. Turn north again through the gate. The farm with the trees on the knoll to the right is Gallowhill, no doubt a former place of execution. Over the rise the path turns off right through a gate and crosses the field north-eastward to the wooded Aydon Dene where it descends to the Cor Burn and up again to Aydon Castle. The early 14th-century fortified house is at the time of writing propped up with scaffolding and timber buttressing and is not open to the public. It has its legends, like most old buildings, often relating to Border rogues and reivers, and one, Jack, gave his name to a vast boulder in the Dene, from which he made a famous leap to freedom.

North past the castle follow the road to the corner, where there is a stone stile in the wall and a public footpath sign pointing to 'Aydon ½'. The path now descends through the trees of the Dene to a new footbridge over the Cor Burn. On the far side it curves up over a fallen tree trunk on a little spur to a small stile in the fence at the top. Now

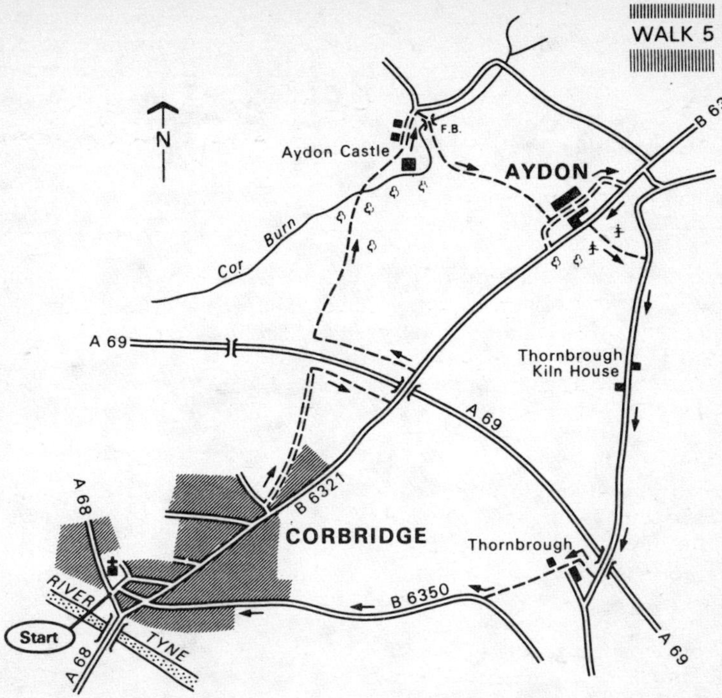

in the open pasture, turn right and follow the edge of the woods above the Cor Burn to just beyond a line of hawthorn trees across the field. Aydon Castle is still impressive on the far steep bank, despite its disfiguring props. Turn left between the twin hillocks beyond the hawthorn hedge and aim for the wide track which leads to the hamlet of Aydon at the end of a line of old knarled trees. At the metalled road walk left and through the hamlet of mellow stone houses and towering trees. Follow the curved road out on the north side to the B6321 and turn right here for a field's distance to where a footpath sign indicates 'High Barns and Newton'. Go through the wide field gate and along the field edge to the double fencing and the two new stiles. Over these the right of way leads diagonally left and slightly uphill through a line of intermittent hawthorn hedge atop an old dyke. Just past this the top of a new footpath sign can be seen at the far corner of the pasture. Aim for this and go out on to the minor road via the strong stile.

Turn right on the road and keep to it for the next mile past the farm and cottage of Thornbrough Kiln, beyond which are the site of old limestone quarries and on the right substantial lime kilns. It is a quiet by-road with little traffic about. It crosses the new A69 by a bridge. Climb the metal barrier (or walk round the far end of it) on the far right side and walk down the edge of the field below using the stiles at either end. Turn left along the lane to the tiny hamlet of Thornbrough and cross straight over at the junction, following the direction of the footpath sign, over the rise straight ahead towards the wooded valley of the Tyne. The path emerges on to the Corbridge road via a kissing gate. Walk westwards back to Corbridge.

Walk 6 — Hexham, Acomb and Anick

9 miles (15 km)

OS sheet 87, grid ref 938643

This walk is on the northern slopes of the Tyne beginning from the main Hexham car park.

Cross the Tyne by the road bridge and go up to the roundabout on the Hexham bypass, the A69; go round it to the north-east side to follow the Oakwood and Anick road uphill to the back of St Camillus' Hospital, the first building on the right.

Use the stone step stile in the wall up on the left. It is signposted to Birkey Burn Road and Acomb. Walk through the little copse round the edge of the cottage garden and out via another stile into the field above. Cross straight over and uphill to a third stile out on to a minor road. Turn left on this and follow it along past the entrance to Target House to the crossroads at Peasley Gates.

From here take the cul-de-sac opposite and, curving round the far side of the grounds of The Riding, walk up to the estate cottages which form a hamlet. Continue north on the bridleway and down to the bridge over the Birkey Burn and up the far bank to Acomb village. Turn left on the main road through the village, past the Miner's Arms, and cross to the north side to follow the lane round the corner of the shop window. Keep to the right of the wall, not into the farmyard, and follow the field edges downhill.

The path descends steeply by steps and turns sharp left to the footbridge over the Red Burn. Cross and turn right up the field beside the trees to the hawthorn hedge above. Go through the gap between the end of the hedge and the wall and up the next field with a fence and hedge and then a wall on the left. There is a gate at the top of this field. Through this go on for a few yards beyond the corner of the field to a new stile. Keep uphill diagonally from this stile going just to the right of the now disused engine house of the old Acomb pit. From the far side of this aim towards Halfway House now visible ahead. The stile out of this section is concealed on the approach side by a holly bush to the left of a gate.

Go out into the lane and along the few yards to the road at Halfway House. Turn right and follow this quiet road uphill past beech and chestnut trees for almost a mile to Fallowfield Farm.

There is a signposted right of way which cuts off a corner before Fallowfield but as the field is arable, it is little further and easier to continue on the road.

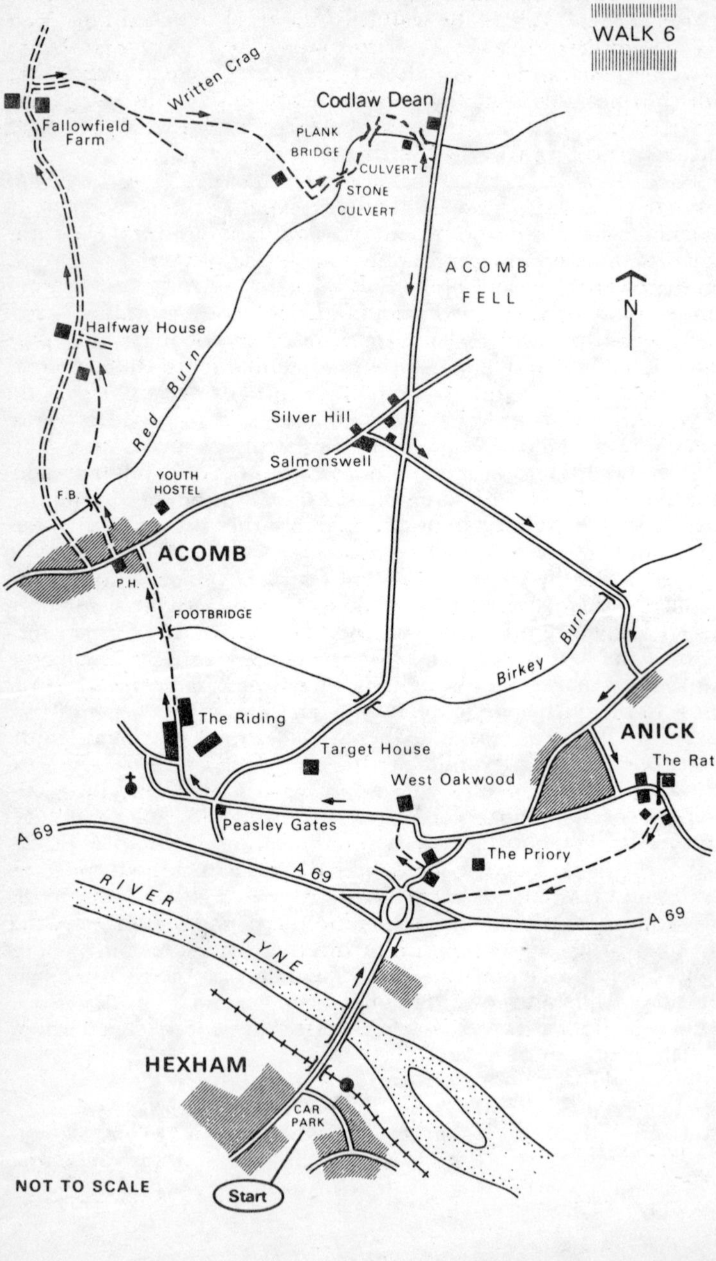
WALK 6
Codlaw Dean
Written Crag
Fallowfield Farm
PLANK BRIDGE
CULVERT
STONE CULVERT
ACOMB FELL
N
Halfway House
Red Burn
Silver Hill
Salmonswell
YOUTH HOSTEL
F.B.
ACOMB
P.H.
FOOTBRIDGE
Birkey Burn
The Riding
Target House
ANICK
The Rat
West Oakwood
Peasley Gates
A 69
The Priory
A 69
RIVER TYNE
A 69
HEXHAM
CAR PARK
Start
NOT TO SCALE

Behind the last barn join the broad clear bridleway signposted to Salmonswell and walk alongside the wall backed by fine tall trees, some limes among them. Where the wall ends the track goes out into open grassland and there are wide views down over the Tyne valley. There is now a wire fence and beyond that on the left an isolated plantation. A path (but not part of today's walk), leads behind this plantation to Written Crag, so-called from a Roman inscription with the words 'Petra Flavi Carantini' carved on the rock slabs.

For today's walk continue on the track to the right of the fence. Through the next gate the track divides. Keep to the main one nearer to the fence. After the next gate there is a wall alongside on the right and a small stone building, probably part of the old mine workings. Continue towards the dene of the Red Burn and turn left at the junction in the woods. Walk upstream among the hawthorn and wild rose to cross where the burn flows under in an old stone culvert. The path climbs gradually towards a field on the right. Ignore the little gate into the field and use the new gap stile ahead. Turn right past the fence which protects an old mine shaft and recross the burn by the bridge made of railway sleepers. The path recrosses the burn over another concealed culvert and comes out to a drive past the back of the cottage and below the farm at Codlaw Dean.

Turn right on the road and go downhill and over the crossroads and downhill again to the next crossroads. Turn left following the indicated direction to Oakwood. This is a very pleasant quiet road with splendid views over the Tyne valley. Continue to the T-junction and turn right where the signpost points to Hexham. At the next junction turn left down to Anick, then left again and round in a curve to just below the Rat, the inn taking its name from a preserved rat on show inside.

Just below the inn a footpath sign to 'Hexham 1½' points south-west. Follow the direction indicated beside the farm buildings, now used by a fencing contractor, and using the smaller of the two gates walk down the fenced-in path into a pasture below. The busy A69 is below on the left. The track is clear on the ground. Follow it gradually down to the far lower corner where there is a broken kissing gate. The track now continues along the bottom of the next field (not inside the wood as shown on the current edition of the 1:50,000 Ordnance Survey map), to a kissing gate into the trees below the grounds of the Priory. The path comes out on to the busy motor road via a new stile in the wooden fence.

Cross over with care and return to Hexham by the road bridge used at the beginning of the walk.

Walk 7 — Swallowship Woods

3 miles (5 km)

OS sheet 87, grid ref 959638

This is a very easy short walk, a morning or afternoon stroll through woodland and along a riverbank.

The parking space is in a lay-by left after road straightening on the road between Corbridge and Hexham on the south side of the Tyne and west of Dilston. If travelling from the Newcastle side look out for the sign 'Car Park ½ ml'. From the Hexham end it is just east of the outskirts past a petrol station.

The path leads from the centre of the parking area between hedges of hawthorn at right-angles to the road and going slightly uphill. Keep to the main track ignoring a fork to the left in the woodland higher up. There is a broken-down wall on the left. The woods are mixed, mainly coniferous plantation but with some oak and silver birch. Continue to the T-junction at Five Gates. The cottage was demolished in 1983. Turn left, then shortly right down a forest ride through Park Plantation. This ride is often very churned up by forestry tractors and can be extremely muddy. Heather and bracken grow alongside and provide a little drier ground where the trees are not too close. Disregard all rides or tracks off to left or right but keep to the main route until it descends almost to the Devil's Water. The river banks are very precipitous at this point and the steep and wooded opposite bank can be seen through a gap in the trees. The main ride turns off at a very sharp angle to the left just before the river's brink. The right of way turns right along what is now a wide ride between two sections of forest planted at two different periods and so at obviously different heights. This is from a point about one hundred yards short of the sharp angle in the main track.

After a short distance there is an open space on the left. It is planted with young trees. At rough cross-tracks the footpath goes over a gap in the broken stone wall and then bears off left towards the river bank and under beautiful old tall pines. Now the path follows the upper rim of the Devil's Water upstream, shortly crossing a little side stream and then passing below a clearing with a cottage. Where the path turns in a curve north there is a diversion worth following to the left to the Robber's Cave. The diversion is narrow and descends fairly steeply to another little burn with stepping stones across, and then between rhododendrons to the open clearing on the small spur

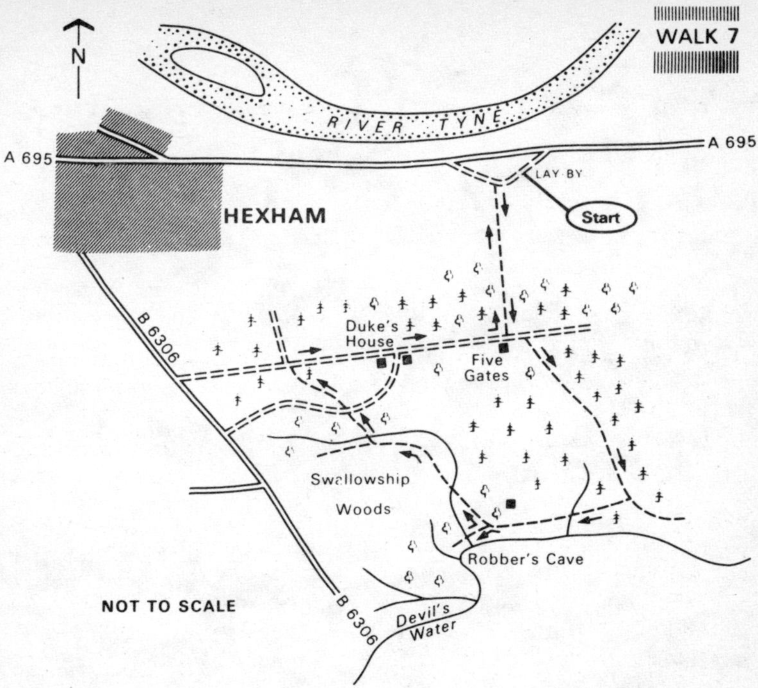

opposite the rock face and huge boulders of the popular picnic area known as the Robber's Cave.

Return to the main original track by retracing the path back to the little burn and the stepping stones and then follow the bank upstream until the path rejoins the track. Turn left and north on this, through the tall Scots pine and the rhododendron bushes to a corner where there is an open field on the left and where a large section of forest has been felled.

Wild flowers abound in this area at the right time of year and in August may be seen such things as knapweed, wild betany, scabious and angelica, bush rose, guelder rose and meadowsweet.

Cross a tiny burn and bear slightly right and north past brambles, goat willow and honeysuckle. Presently the path curves west and there is a branch off north and down over a dip. Follow this latter track towards an old wall and to the left along this. The ground is often very muddy under the trees here and walkers have made various routes to avoid this. The tracks converge towards a road, flanked by majestic Californian redwoods. Cross straight over and continue north to the next surfaced road. Turn right on this and walk east past the multi-chimneyed Dukes House to Five Gates Cottage again and back down the footpath left to the lay-by on the main road.

Walk 8 — Hexham, West Dipton Burn and Hole House

7 miles (11 km)

OS sheet 87, grid ref 938643

There is ample parking space at Hexham. The walk is described from the main car and coach park below the town on the north side. It is seven miles long but can be shortened to five or three at suitable stages.

Leave the car park by the western exit and walk up to the town market place and across it to Beaumont Street past the Abbey and park. Cross over the main east-west road through the town and go up past the stone terraced houses of St Wilfred's Road to the junction at the entrance gate to Haining, Croft. Turn right up the little hill and pass the ends of Elverston Road and St Andrew's Road and along the walled lane ahead. There is the dene of a little burn beyond the corner of the castellated wall. Turn left and walk upstream, keeping to the east bank under a walled bankside until the path crosses the burn by a stone bridge.

The path now rises to a children's playground and circles it to the left above the burn. Pass the heavily railed 'under twelves' playground and the pigeon lofts. Just before reaching the housing estate turn left and follow the narrow path along the garden edges and below a small reservoir embankment. Through the kissing gate keep to the path which presently approaches the water's edge and then comes out on to a minor road.

Turn left and follow this as it curves round between houses and gardens and becomes an unsurfaced track going straight uphill to Intake Farm. Opposite the farm is a kissing gate into a field. Leave the lane and walk along the lower edge of the field above the wooded dene for rather less than a hundred yards to where a stile, partially concealed by a hawthorn, leads the path into the wood.

Turn left under a holly tree and follow the little valley upstream, not crossing the burn, as the path appears to do at an early stage, but keeping to the same bank and using the narrow track among the trees not far from the left-hand perimeter fence. A good stile provides egress from the wood. Continue upstream among the gorse bushes to emerge on to a minor road beside a public footpath sign pointing back to Intake Farm.

Walk uphill on the straight narrow road past Benson's Fell and the entrance to Causey Hill caravan site to the junction on the High

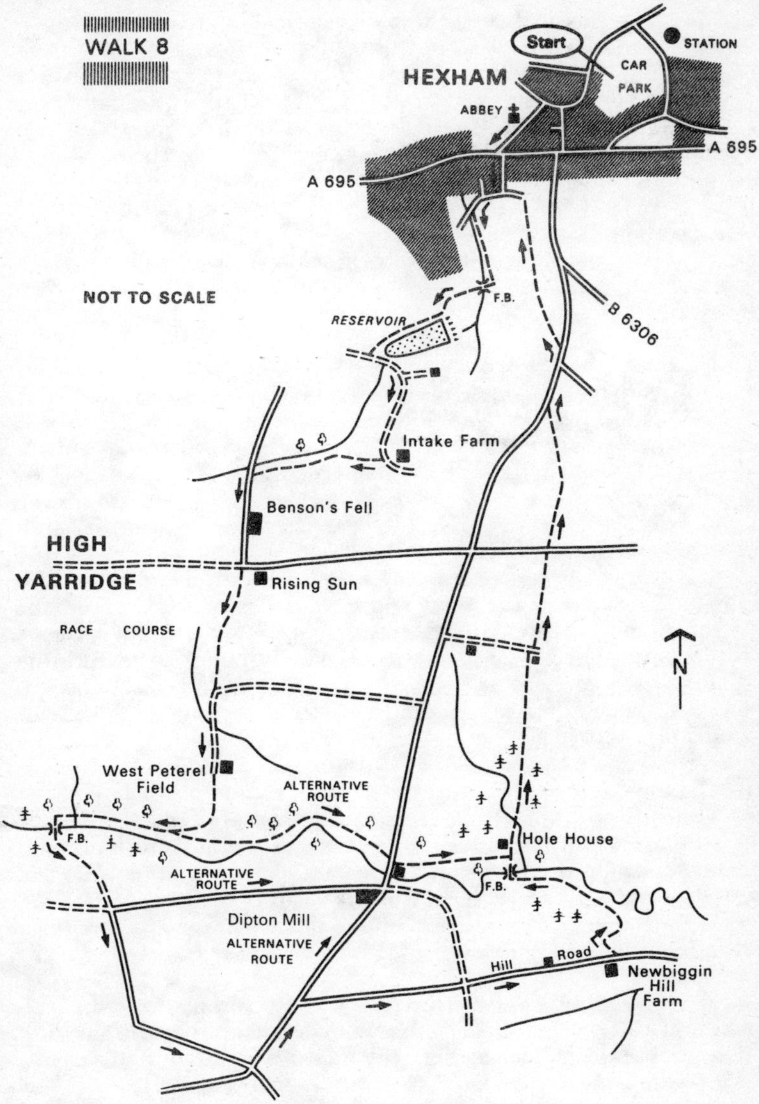
WALK 8
HEXHAM
Start
STATION
CAR
PARK
ABBEY
A 695
A 695
NOT TO SCALE
F.B.
B 6306
RESERVOIR
Intake Farm
Benson's Fell
HIGH
YARRIDGE
Rising Sun
RACE COURSE
N
West Peterel
Field
ALTERNATIVE
ROUTE
F.B.
Hole House
ALTERNATIVE
ROUTE
F.B.
Dipton Mill
ALTERNATIVE
ROUTE
Hill Road
Newbiggin
Hill
Farm

Yarridge road and the whitewashed cottage called the Rising Sun. Cross straight over to the stile and the footpath on the right of the cottage taking the direction indicated by the signpost down the edge of the field. In the next field the path bears off a little to the right and goes diagonally across almost to the far south-west corner where there is a stile beside a wide field gate. The Hexham race-course and its stands are just to the west now. In the next field the path goes due south and parallel to the field edges. It is broad and clear on the ground on a raised section. Over the next stile to the right of a gate the land dips away to the south towards the valley of the Dipton Burn.

The farm ahead is West Peterel Field and the route uses the lane which passes to the right of this. Continue down the field edge south of the farm with the hedge and fence on the right but, halfway down the next field, cross the stile beside the gate into the field on the right and proceed downhill with the field boundary now on the left. Shortly the track goes into the woods of the West Dipton Burn valley and turns upstream. After it descends to the valley bottom there is a choice of return routes. Downstream and eastward is the shorter. The path is narrow and somewhat muddy in wet weather and comes out on to the road beside the pub at Dipton Mill.

Right and upstream is now described. The final section of all the variations is the same from Hole House near the Dipton Mill pub and is described at the end.

Follow the valley bottom through the oak and mixed woodland to the footbridge over the West Dipton Burn; cross and ascend the far bank on the wide track. At the road above there is another choice of return routes. Left is Dipton Mill. Ahead a quiet road extends the walk.

For the longer route follow the road south, turning left just over the Nicholas Burn and then left again on the Dipton Mill road. At the first junction either continue on to the pub and mill house (converted and modernised), and take the path on the north side of the burn eastwards to Hole House; or turn right before Dipton Mill and follow this quiet and rather pretty road east as far as Newbiggin Hill Farm, the second dwelling but first group of farm buildings on the right. Just opposite the east end of the farm is a gate leading to a zig-zag path down to the West Dipton Burn. Descend to the burn and walk upstream to the footbridge below Hole House. Cross to the north side.

Hole House is the point on the return route common to all variations of the walk. It is a short distance downstream from Dipton Mill.

The path passes close to the right side of the house between the garden wall and a tall hedge. From the back corner it crosses a tiny burn and goes up through the woods due north. It is well used and quite clear on the ground. It emerges from the wood via a wicket gate, and keeps straight on by the edge of the fields until it comes parallel to Queen's Letch Farm and near a small disused building, where there is a signpost pointing back to Newbiggin. Both stile and gate are rather awkward. Use either and then continue due north again with field boundaries now on the left.

The route crosses straight over the minor road at the top of the hill and the path descends towards Hexham along the field edges. There are wide views ahead over the Tyne valley.

Turn downhill at the road on the outskirts of Hexham. To finish the last stretch away from the noise and smell of traffic, cross to the left side at the junction with the Blanchland road and turn off down the snicket just beside the garden of the end house of Elverston Drive. The narrow lonnen between walls is known locally as The Cut and it descends parallel to the road and behind the houses, gardens and hospital. It comes out beside the entrance gate of Haining Croft at the top of St Wilfred's Road and the beginning of the walk.

Walk 9 Steel, Whitley Chapel and Peth Foot

5 miles (8 km)

OS sheet 87, grid ref 938585

This field, woodland and riverside walk in the heart of Hexhamshire has easy gradients and is well sheltered. It can be easily divided into two short walks if required.

There is a good parking area on the roadside close to and on the south side of the Rowley Burn between Dye House and Steel Farm about five miles due south of Hexham and roughly west of Slaley.

Walk west along the riverside path on the south side of the Rowley Burn, through the natural woodland backed by mature plantings of tall Scots pine. Continue upstream into more closely planted younger spruce trees to where the path forks. Take the left fork away from the burn and slightly uphill to the edge of the plantation where there is a new stile into a field. (This is a recent slight diversion from the right of way as shown on the Ordnance Survey map. The original path continues along the Rowley Burn to a side stream and can still be used but is subject to flooding.)

Walk to the right along the field edge for a few yards and cross a second stile right again into the plantation by the stream. Step left over the stream and climb a third stile. This realigns the route and leads west to Mollersteads. The path follows the fence and hawthorn hedge to a staggered corner and then bears gradually across to the second gate on the right and through that up again towards the farm. The right of way is through the left of two gates on the left of the big barn, but a stile under a tree to the side of the approach route leads into the field on the south side of Mollersteads, the same field which carries the right of way south from the farm.

Walk south along the nearside base of the knoll of oak trees, through a wide wooden gate and on alongside a hawthorn hedge to another gate. The back of the whitewashed Click'em Inn, also more correctly called the Fox and Hounds, at Whitley Chapel is visible ahead and the path aims directly to the back of this via more gates. A little gate with yellow painted markings leads into the garden. Walk left round the inn through the car park and out on to the road in front.

The walk continues a short distance west from here to the crossroads beside the schoolhouse and the chapel on its little mound. Turn left following the signposted direction towards Lilswood and Harwood Shield and left again past the churchyard through the field gate (not

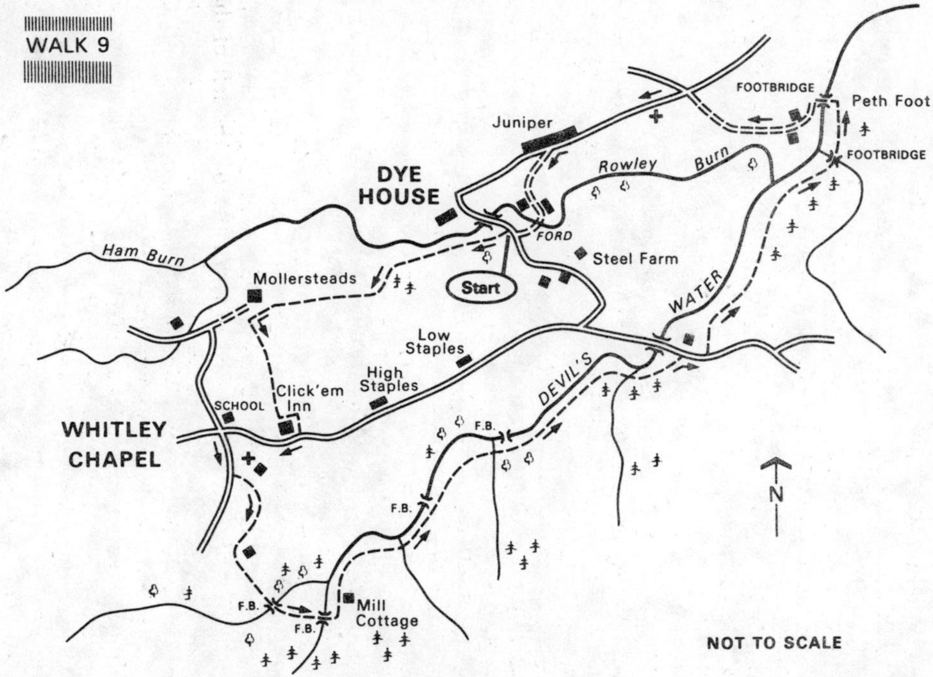
WALK 9
FOOTBRIDGE
Peth Foot
Juniper
FOOTBRIDGE
Rowley Burn
DYE HOUSE
FORD
Steel Farm
Ham Burn
Mollersteads
Start
WATER
Low Staples
High Staples
DEVIL'S
Click'em Inn
SCHOOL
WHITLEY CHAPEL
F.B.
F.B.
N
F.B.
Mill Cottage
F.B.
NOT TO SCALE

the garden gate beside it) and along the edge of the rough boggy pasture towards the farm south of the chapel. At the approach to the farm turn right, not into the farm enclosure but through the field gate past the telegraph pole to the right of the metal barn, then left down the edge of the field past the side of the farm and towards the woods in the valley of the Devil's Water.

The stone stile into the woods is at the extreme left end of the low stone wall where it joins the fence. The path is well marked in the trees. Follow it down to a wooden footbridge over a little tributary burn then up over a rise. Ignore branches off to the right from the top of the rise and descend by the main path to the concrete and metal footbridge over the Devil's Water.

A wide track descends from the forest on the right on the south side and leads towards Mill Cottage. Follow it along the field and through the gate to the left of the cottage and on downstream along the Devil's Water. It is a clear wide track through meadows and gorse-grown pasture and woodland. It passes two footbridges, useful for future reference but not part of today's walk, decaying arched buildings, and part of an old smelt mill at the bottom of the track down from Dukesfield, and comes out on to the road a short distance south of Steel Farm.

The starting point is half a mile along the road to the left if a shorter route is required. To continue the longer route turn right up the hill and join the track in the small enclosure above the cottage opposite. The wide field gate opens on to a delightful walk beside tall waving Scots pines which top the bankside above the Devil's Water. Continue into the plantation where the wide track narrows to a footpath and descends gradually to a footbridge over a tributary burn, then down to the recently rebuilt Peth Foot bridge, rebuilt after the old footbridge was washed away in floods.

Cross the Devil's Water to the north side, then left and follow the track which becomes a surfaced lane between the imposing modern dwelling and the Peth Foot Cottage. Continue up to the crossroads near Ordley and turn left following the sign post direction to Dye House. Towards the end of the line of cottages at Juniper an interesting little short cut leads down left below the road to cottages and a ford over the Rowley Burn. A concrete walkway over the burn is provided for pedestrians. The short cut emerges on to the Steel road just opposite the parking space.

The village shop on the north side of the Rowley Burn has ice-cream and soft drinks among other commodities available. The name Dye House is to be taken literally. Dyes were made from mallows grown at Mollersteads and used for the once flourishing glove-making industry of Hexham.

Walk 10
5½ miles (9 km)

Blanchland via Pennypie and Bulbeck Common

OS sheet 87, grid ref 964504

The village of Blanchland is one of the most picturesque in the county. Built in a square extending from one corner of the Abbey, part of which is incorporated into the Lord Crewe Hotel, it retains the mellowness of stone and the atmosphere of the early medieval period. It stands on the north bank of the Derwent, which marks the boundary between Northumberland and Durham.

There is a large car park to the north side of the village, on the road to Pennypie House. Leave the car here and follow the road north along the Shildon Burn under the tall pines, past the cottages and remnants of the old lead mining industry, past the new barn and on up to Pennypie. It is said that miners carrying the ore over the moor to the Carriers' Way used to buy a pie for a penny from this farm.

Just past the house go through the gate and turn right and uphill. There is still rough pasture over the wall on the right. Go through the gate and out on to the moor at the top. Look for the wide metal gate about 50 yards on, on the left. Go through this gate and follow the track west and just above the wall for over a mile until the land dips down towards the valley of the Devil's Water. The large declivities in the moor are old quarry workings. A few yards below these is a gate in the wall on the left. This marks the line of the Carriers' Way, the route used for transporting the lead ore from the mines of upper Allendale to Slaley and thence to the Tyne. The route, although much overgrown, is discernible on the ground, a levelled track running in an obvious hollow for much of its length. Follow it through the gate and south, contouring above the valley which is now below on the right.

The wide moor all round is part of Bulbeck Common and is rather featureless. Without a compass it would be difficult to be sure of the route and advisable to retrace one's steps in misty conditions. In clear weather the Carriers' Way aims towards a small stone bothy visible ahead on the far slope of the little tributary valley of the Black Burn which flows north-west into the Devil's Water. It passes en route a small wooden platform on a green stretch of turf. This is a feeding place for sheep. Further on it has been cut across during the laying of gas pipelines. The land has been reinstated but is still recognisable as a somewhat gravelly stretch. There is an inspection valve in the

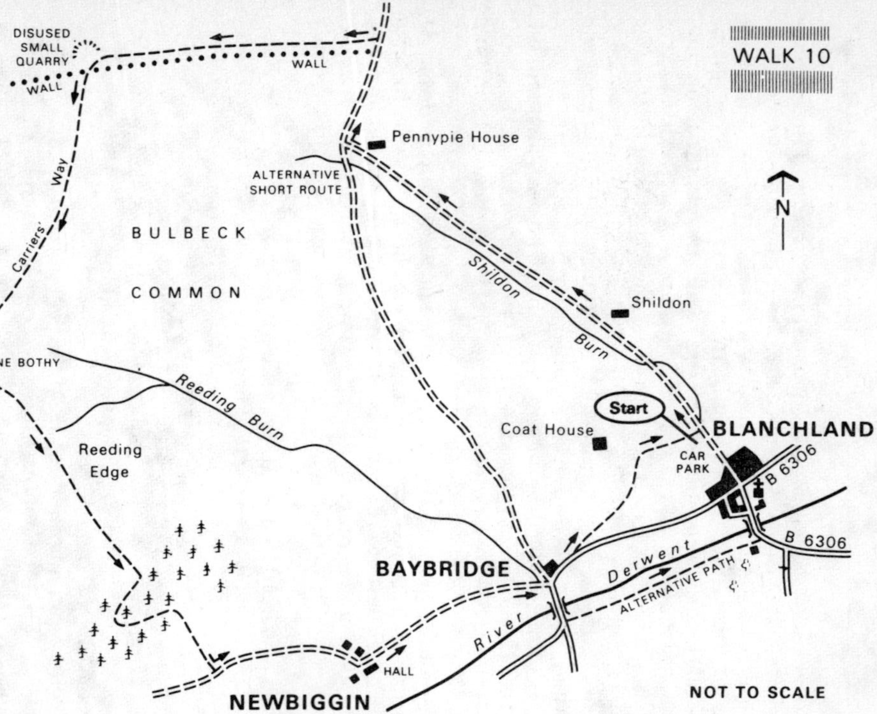
WALK 10
N
DISUSED
SMALL
QUARRY
WALL
WALL
Pennypie House
ALTERNATIVE
SHORT ROUTE
Carriers' Way
BULBECK
COMMON
Shildon Burn
Shildon
STONE BOTHY
Reeding Burn
Reeding
Edge
Start
Coat House
BLANCHLAND
CAR
PARK
B 6306
B 6306
BAYBRIDGE
River Derwent
ALTERNATIVE PATH
HALL
NEWBIGGIN
NOT TO SCALE

centre and a cairn on the far side. The stone bothy is marked clearly on the Ordnance Survey map. Keep to the right of the enclosure round it and join the clear track on the south side. Turn left and go through the gate on the slight rise. Several tracks lead off from here. Take that which leads south-east diagonally from the gate rising slightly over Reeding Edge to the western hill above the Reeding Burn. It is a good clear track on the ground. Follow it over the moor and into the plantation of Whitehill, above the Derwent valley.

It is not possible at present to follow the right of way through the plantation as the trees grow too closely together at the lower part. The forest road is slightly longer but arrives at the same point. Follow it west for a space, then in a curve down left to a gate at a point below the entrance into the plantation. (The line of the right of way is indicated by the tiny stile at the edge of the wood just inside the gate.) Go through the gate into the field and turn right immediately and down to the bottom corner. There are two gates here. The upper is on the correct line of the right of way and leads down on the far side of the descending wall to the Newbiggin road visible below. Turn left and follow this road past Newbiggin House and Hall and on to Baybridge.

Join the motor road at the corner and follow it east to Blanchland. As it is sometimes rather busy in the summer and without pavement or grass verge, it is pleasanter to take the path through the fields and back to the car park. To do this look for the gate up on the left one field along after passing the cottages at Baybridge. The path climbs diagonally up the field to near the top corner and then joins the farm road coming down from Coat House. Turn right on to this road and follow it out on to the Shildon road where the walk began. The car park is just below on the right.

Walk 11 — Carts Bog and Staward Pele

5 miles (8 km)

OS sheet 87, grid ref 818605

This walk on the eastern banks of the Allen south of Plankey Mill includes some of the finest views in the county. The parking area is along the side road near the Carts Bog Inn (also known as the Green Tree) on the Hexham to Alston road, the A686.

Walk north along the A686 from the Inn and in about 40 yards fork left on to a minor road signposted to Lough Green, Plankey Mill and Bardon Mill. Continue on this minor road past a single-storey dwelling on the right, down a little dip to where the fields appear rather swampy and curving up on the far slope to where there are plantations on either side, silver birch, Scots pine, and near the recessed gate to Harsondale, a few tall sycamore and beech.

Turn left off the minor road over the cattle grid on to the Harsondale Farm road. The tall pine trees are now on the right. Walk west towards the main Allen river; the valley of the West Allen opening out in the far left, the old Staward Station and the ruined farm of Gingle Pot on the nearer hillside, whose bulk conceals the deep East Allen valley.

Pass a second plantation of mixed conifers and look for a new ladder stile at the far end of the field on the right. Harsondale Farm is now in view. Climb the stile and go northwards up the edge of the field beside the wall and climb the stone step stile in the top corner. In the next field the path continues between the wall and a line of hawthorn trees. There is a small derelict stone building ahead. Beyond this the land slopes down towards Sillywray Farm and there is another stone stile in the wall.

Over on the far northern horizon is the long escarpment of the Whinsill carrying Hadrian's Wall on its summit, from the Nine Nicks of Thirlwall (near Greenhead) in the west to the crags near Sewing Shields in the east.

Go through the wooden field-gate just before Sillywray and keeping alongside the wall bear right towards the barn, through a metal gate and on to the farm road. Continue east for a short distance past the arched hemmel, a multi-purpose barn, as far as the side road off to the north again. This is a hard surfaced rough road between walls and leads into fields again via a wide metal gate. Keep the wall on the right and walk alongside it to the stream, the Linn Burn, which

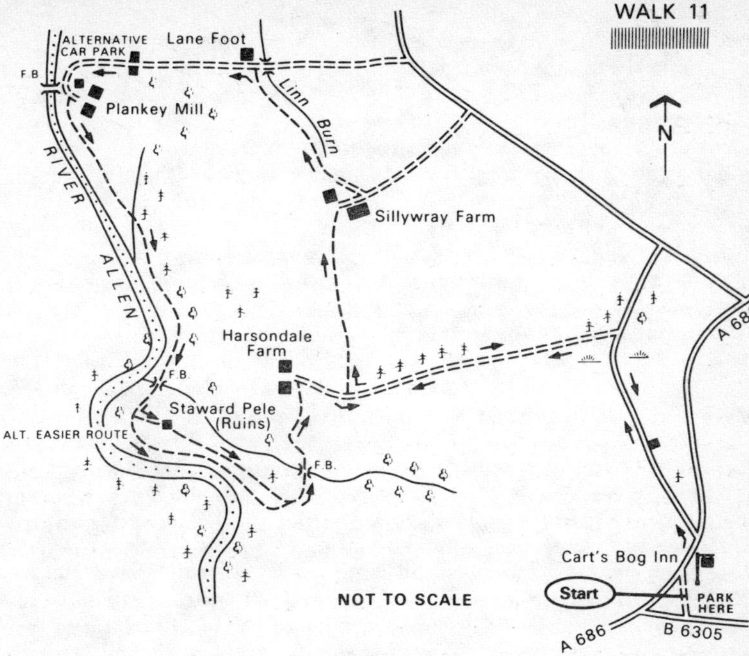

descends ahead into a wooded dene. Skirt the left perimeter of this and walk down towards the modernised cottage of Lane Foot on the Plankey Mill road.

There is a new stile near the low stone parapet of the road bridge over the Linn Burn. Turn left on the road and walk down to the river Allen at Plankey Mill.

This is a popular parking and picnic area at weekends and holidays whenever the weather is reasonable, and some refreshments of the pop and ice-cream variety are available at the farm.

As the present walk is all on the east side of the Allen do not cross the suspension bridge but continue upstream from the end of it, along the river bank and into the flat meadow on the approach to the wooded section. A wide metal gate leads to the woodland path. After about 200 yards the path rises gradually as the banks steepen. Branch paths to the right lead to the riverside only and do not continue. Much further on the path descends again and crosses the Harsondale Burn over a small wooden footbridge.

The Harsondale Burn spills into the Allen from a steep-sided wooded cleugh below Harsondale Farm. The Allen flows from the south in an equally deep wooded gorge which provides the magnificent view familiar to all travellers on the A686, Hexham to Alston road on the way down to the Cupola Bridge near Whitfield. The high narrow spur of land between the two valleys is the site of a ruined medieval pele tower. Long after it was abandoned as a stronghold it is reputed to have been used as a hideout for local freebooters and cattle thieves. The Thief's Loup in the Harsondale was so-called to commemorate an escapade of one such.

Although there is little now left of the Staward Pele it is well worth making the steep ascent of the spur for views of the Allen gorge and the Harsondale cleugh. After the footbridge the path turns right for a few yards, then curves left and forks. The right fork goes to the riverside. Take the left and after a few more yards where again the track forks take the uphill left fork to reach the top of the spur. For those who dislike the exertion of a steep climb the path which goes on round the base of the spur climbs gradually to the same open grass area as the Staward Pele route but the views are less exciting. The steep path is in no way alarming. There are plenty of small tree branches, bilberry bushes and clumps of heather to clutch if the feet slip. The path is often muddy. At the top is the west facing wall of the tower. The inner part can be reached from either side.

Leave Staward Pele east along the ridge past what is left of the gatehouse. The ridge is only a few feet wide and the views are impressive. **The path emerges from the woodland via a wooden stile into a big open field. Continue in the same general direction over the rise** to a wide gate in the opposite wall leading back into the woods and plantings of the upper Harsondale Cleugh. (The alternative path which omits Staward Pele comes across the field to the same gate.)

From the gate the path descends through the conifers to the burn. Apart from a boggy section where it bears left along the edge it is quite distinct. There is a fine new footbridge over the Harsondale Burn at the bottom. It replaces an old one damaged in floods a year or two ago. The burn is full of boulders and broken branches, the debris of frequent flooding in this narrow cleugh. The path ascends to the left on the far side and a wicket gate at the upper edge of the woods leads out into the field below Harsondale Farm. Climb directly **up the field to a ladder stile to the right of the farm buildings and come out on to the farm road near the beginning of the walk.**

The fine old stone farm occupies a splendid hill site facing south over the Harsondale to the Allen valley and the old lead bearing hills around.

Turn right along the farm lane and retrace the route back to Carts Bog.

Walk 12 Allenbanks

3 or 5 miles (5 or 8 km)

OS sheet 87, grid ref 797640

From the confluence of its east and west tributaries, the Allen scrambles over rocks and boulders through a deep and wooded gorge to join the South Tyne near Ridley.

There are two good car parks and one is free. It has been provided by the National Trust who now own the lower reaches of the Allen, and can be approached by turning off the A69 one mile east of Bardon Mill and branching left before the entrance gates to Ridley Hall. The car park and picnic area occupy the site of the old walled garden on the west bank of the Allen close to Moralee Bridge. The other parking area is at Plankey Mill, about one-and-a-half miles upstream on the east bank. It is sited on a flat haugh by the river on private land and is more suitable for those who want to stay all day in one place. The route is described from the National Trust car park.

Walk out by the main entrance and turn right along the road and over the bridge. Here on the left is the National Trust sign indicating the footpath to Allenbanks and a wicket gate. Go down under the bridge and follow the Allen upstream close to the river. Beyond the first meadow the route enters Moralee Woods, the old overgrown parkland of Ridley Hall, with rhododendrons among the tall pines.

There are several paths through the woods. Keep to the lowest near the river. Do not cross by the first suspension bridge. Stay on the east bank and continue upstream on the main track to the southern limits of the wood. Cross the Linn Burn by the footbridge and then a stile leading on to flat grassland where a wire fence on the left is replaced further on by the traditional dry stone wall.

The steep valley sides seem to have been pushed back on the east side. They rise up beyond the Linn Burn. Perhaps the Allen has altered course, cutting a new and straighter bed and leaving this flat haugh in the valley bottom.

Come into the meadow by the next stile and climb the muddy track ahead to another stile between the old ruined buildings and the river. Join the rough road beyond the buildings and turn right and up on to the metalled road above Plankey Mill. Now turn right and downhill to the farm and car park and cross the main Allen river by the long swaying suspension bridge. This is the furthest point of the walk. The return route follows the west bank. Keep fairly close to the river

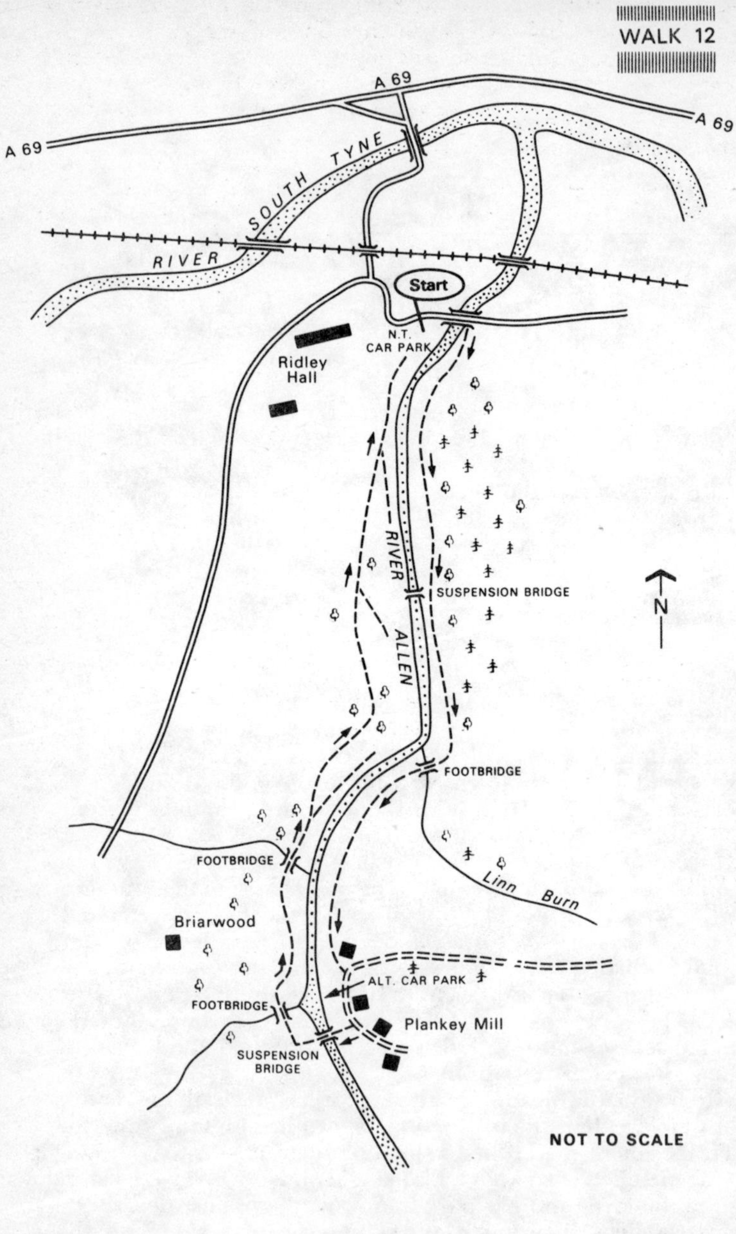

WALK 12
A 69
A 69
A 69
RIVER SOUTH TYNE
Start
N.T. CAR PARK
Ridley Hall
RIVER ALLEN
SUSPENSION BRIDGE
N
FOOTBRIDGE
Linn Burn
FOOTBRIDGE
Briarwood
ALT. CAR PARK
FOOTBRIDGE
Plankey Mill
SUSPENSION BRIDGE
NOT TO SCALE

on the main path, crossing the Kingswood Burn by the wooden footbridge. Another side stream further on is spanned by four railway sleepers. About a hundred yards beyond this the track forks, the lower keeping to the riverside and returning directly to the car park; the other rising to the upper edge of the woods and giving more open views and a possible extension to the walk if required.

This upper route comprises a steepish rise at the outset and then a pleasant flat stretch between the well spaced silvery trunks of tall beech trees before descending to the open grass parkland fronting Ridley Hall. At this point there is a National Park sign. This is the point of departure for the extension to the tiny hamlet of Beltingham. To return to the car park from here, continue straight ahead to a fence and stile leading into a private section of the grounds. Do not cross the stile but turn down right following the stepped path into the southern end of the picnic site and parking area.

For the extension to Beltingham hamlet cross the stile by the sign and follow the line of trees along the edge of the Hall grounds to the stile, kissing gate and farm track out on to the road. Turn left and walk as far as the junction where the signpost indicates 'Beltingham ½ mile', and follow it to the hamlet. The church, with its lych-gate, ancient yew trees (that on the north side thought to be 900 years old) and small burial ground for members of the Bowes-Lyon family, was one of the many resting places for the monks from Lindisfarne on their long journey with the remains of Saint Cuthbert, which they were safeguarding from marauding Danes. The martyred Bishop Ridley was baptized here. He was born in this area, probably at Willimonstwick, now a farm with an ancient pele tower, about a mile to the west.

To continue the journey, walk a few yards south from the lych-gate and take the green lonnen with a Victoria Regina post box. Following the direction indicated by the footpath sign to 'Ridley Bridge and Allenbanks', go down to the Beltingham Burn and cross to a gate. Keeping due east follow the fenced track back to the road near Ridley. Turn left and walk down to the road junction near the main entrance to Ridley Hall. Now take the road round to the right outside the edge of the grounds back to the car park.

Walk 13 — Featherstone and Kellah

4 miles (6.5 km)

OS sheet 86, grid ref 673614

This walk among the woods and fields of the South Tyne Valley begins from any suitable point along the quiet roadside between Park Burnfoot Farm and the entrance to Featherstone Castle grounds.

Walk across Featherstone road bridge to the north side and look for the old-fashioned 'ladies' stile' about 20 yards on, on the left. This leads to a good clear path through the woods beside the South Tyne. Shortly after crossing the Glencune Burn by the little footbridge look for the blue painted County footbridge over the South Tyne but do not cross. Turn right and up by the half-hidden wooden steps to the top of the wood and out into the field above. There are further steps up here. Continue uphill past the cottage of Horse Close and on to the corner of a wire mesh fence. Keep alongside this to the wayside calvary in its small enclosure. The cottage along the road to the right is Maiden Way House, the road here coinciding with the Roman Maiden Way.

Cross the road from the kissing gate and climb the wooden palings beside the concrete marker post opposite and walk up the field edges alongside the fence. The hamlet of Kellah is two field lengths away.

At Kellah turn left in front of the cottages and go through the stile in the wall. Turn right, then almost immediately left between the farm buildings, via two gates close together, then straight on across a narrow field, through a gap and downhill to the deep little dene of one of the tributaries of the Kellah Burn. Cross by the wooden footbridge some yards downstream from the right-hand wall. Curve round the spur ahead to another footbridge over the Kellah Burn.

Cross the Kellah Burn and climb the bank on the far side. From the top of the bank cross the field to the line of trees (from a distance there seem to be only two), goat willow, silver birch, and hawthorn, and go over the tiny gap stile near the left hand end of the wall. The top stone on this stile is loose so care is needed. The farm ahead is Ulpham and the group to the right is Baty's Shield. Both are on the Pennine Way. Go up to Ulpham, through a wide field gate and between the farm buildings. Bear left and go through a metal gate, turn right and cross the corner of the field and through a gap between a fence and a wall. Now turn immediately left and keep alongside the fence.

WALK 13

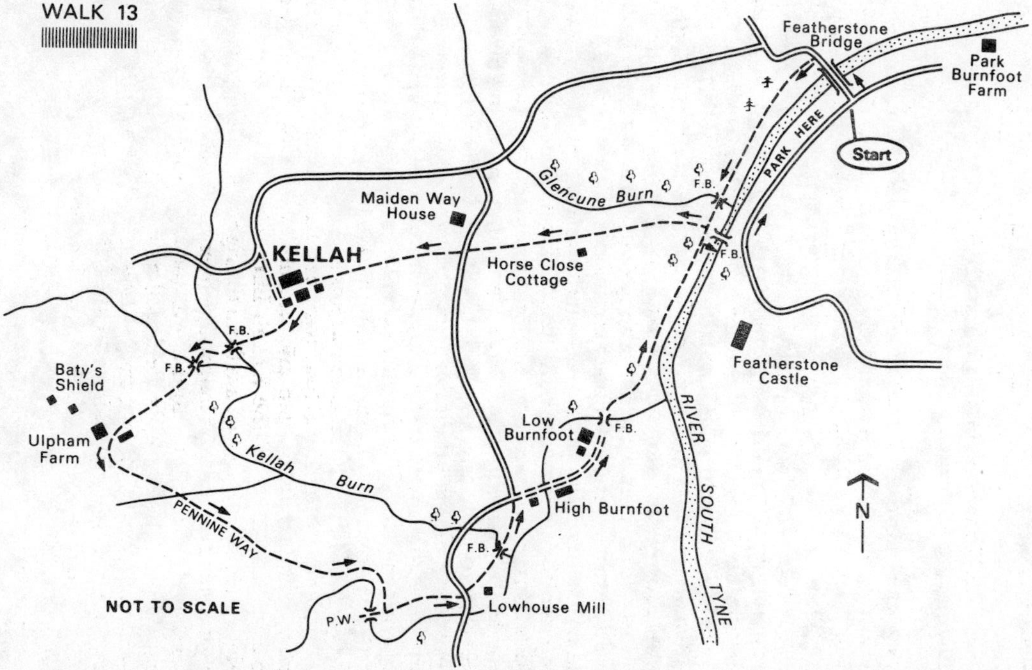

Featherstone Bridge
Park Burnfoot Farm
Start
PARK HERE
F.B.
Glencune Burn
Maiden Way House
KELLAH
Horse Close Cottage
Featherstone Castle
F.B.
F.B.
Baty's Shield
Ulpham Farm
Kellah Burn
Low Burnfoot
F.B.
RIVER SOUTH TYNE
High Burnfoot
PENNINE WAY
F.B.
N
P.W.
Lowhouse Mill
NOT TO SCALE

The 1 : 25 000 Ordnance Survey map shows the path on the left of the field boundary. The fence is more recent than the last map revision and the old field boundary is in evidence a little further on, in the form of a line of hawthorn on top of a crumbling grass grown wall.

This is the Pennine Way. Continue south-east until the land dips to a stream, and climb the rather awkwardly tilted Pennine Way stile beyond. Turn up the far bank aiming gradually towards the long wall on the right. Ignore the first gate and use the second which is close to the point where a fence replaces the wall. Through this continue alongside a fence by spaced hawthorn trees and one fine oak to a loop in the Hartley Burn, alongside which the path descends to a flat meadow haugh via a new stile.

Here the Pennine Way turns off right and crosses the Hartley Burn by a County footbridge. Today's walk joins a path from this bridge in the middle of the meadow and turns sharp left towards a small stone building, Lowhouse Mill, on the roadside opposite the gate out of this meadow.

Cross the road and take the path to the left of the Mill, keeping to the edge of the field and crossing a footbridge over the Kellah Burn. Over a poor broken stile go diagonally over the next field keeping to the base of a steep little bank and come out via a gap (hopefully soon a stile) where the fence has been broken. This is exactly at a road junction. Turn right and follow the minor road, a cul-de-sac, over the flat road-bridge across the burn, past High Burnfoot and on to Low Burnfoot, a very attractive 17th-century house.

Shortly beyond this cross the burn again via the footbridge and follow the path downstream along the South Tyne banks, where wild flowers grow abundantly in season. There are fine views of Featherstone Castle across the river a short distance ahead and the track returns to the County footbridge seen early in the walk. Cross the South Tyne by this to return to the parking space.

Walk 14 — The Tarset Burn

7 miles (11 km)

OS sheet 80, grid ref 776858

The Tarset Burn is a tributary of the North Tyne. This walk is at the fringe of the vast Kielder Forest, a few miles below the Kielder Reservoir.

There is parking space on the curve of road at the tiny hamlet of Hott, by-passed by road straightening and close to the North Tyne, five miles west of Bellingham. The tall parapets of the footbridge over the North Tyne can be seen from Hott.

Cross the main road and go through the left of two wide gates and walk down the field edge to cross the footbridge. Notice the little arched stairway on the north side. Turn left along the riverside path under the trees and join a road near Thorneyburn Station. The railway is disused. Continue west on the road beside the wide meadow haugh. The North Tyne makes a marked loop south here but the road goes straight on. Pass Low Thorneyburn Farm and Thorneyburn Cottage, cross the Thorney Burn on the road bridge and go through the first wide field gate on the right.

Walk at right-angles away from the road, cross the disused railway and climb the hilly pasture ahead. It seems equally populated by sheep and rabbits. There are trees at either side. Over the first rise another summit appears, with the appropriately named Hill House on top of it. Go up to the left of the garden where broom and lilac vie with wild rose and bluebells and through a gap in the wall to the rim of a deep little gorge beyond. Follow the wall and fence for about 150 yards to a gate and through it continue still on the side of the gorge. Two deep valleys with a spur between meet just here. The nearer is that of Deep Sike. Continue along this until a clear track approaches from an angle in the fence on the left and crosses Deep Sike. Turn right on this and follow it over the Sike, over another tiny burn and north-east across the open moor towards the much deeper cleft made by the Thorney Burn. The track is quite clear through the heather and there is a drainage ditch beside it.

Before long there is a line of broken wall ahead. This marks the line of an old broad walled track running across the moor from east to west. It crosses the Thorney Burn at Slaty Ford. The continuation of this walk is through a gap in the wall of this track a few yards west of Slaty Ford. An old stone gatepost marks the opening.

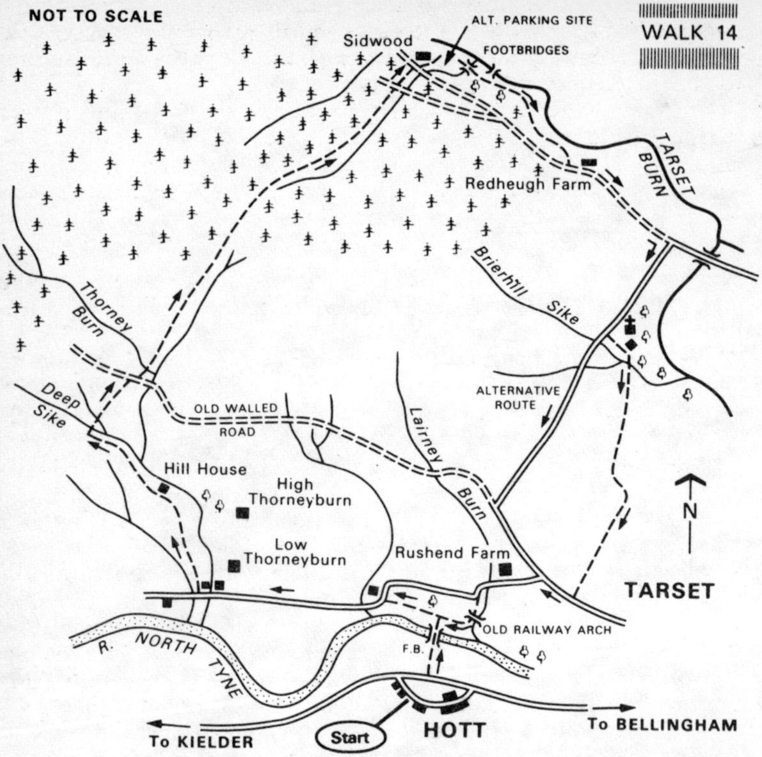

Cross the Thorney Burn beyond this gap and follow the distinct path over the moor. Towards the forest there is a dry stone wall on the right. Go through the gate and alongside the trees. There appear to be various routes from the corner in front of the formidable barricade-like mass of plantings ahead. Bear briefly right then continue in the same general direction as before along a forest ride. Presently the land slopes away ahead towards the valley of the Tarset Burn.

At the junction of rides there is a stream trickling down on the left. Cross this and then turn right to continue in the same direction downhill alongside a stream in a drainage ditch. At another crossing of rides go over a ditch and straight on. The farmlands on the far bank of Tarset Burn are now visible. The ride curves a little further on, but cross over at the next crossing of rides and continue down towards the valley. At the forest road near the valley floor cross to a footpath almost opposite and go down through tall pines to the picnic site and the house at Sidwood.

From the left side of the picnic site go down some steps to follow the waymarked forestry path downstream along the Tarset Burn. This is

a delightful path. It crosses a side stream over a little footbridge. Do not cross the Tarset Burn footbridge shortly after but continue on the west bank following the red waymarks until the path comes out to the road near Redheugh Farm.

Continue on the road south from here. At the junction turn right in the direction of Thorneyburn and walk as far as the church. There is a choice of routes from here; either to continue along the road and turn left at the T-junction to the point where a signpost points to Rushend; or to use the footpath which turns off just past the churchyard. The footpath is not a short-cut and may present some problems in the form of missing stiles and bulls among the cattle.

To use the footpath go through the gate on the left past the churchyard and walk along almost to the end of the ridge in the field then down to the corner where there is new fencing. Climb the fence with care and cross the stream – the Brierhill Sike – and climb the far bank bearing left a little on a narrow path. Cross the wide grassland on top of the bank going gradually away from the sike and aiming towards a remnant of stone ruin, probably a cottage, to a stile in a wire fence not far from the corner.

Cross the next big field diagonally to a clump of conifers towards the south-west. The wall ahead near the trees should have a stile or gate to allow passage into the field next to the plantation, but by using a gate to the left and then two gates at the near end of the trees it is possible to get into the field containing the public footpath. This is a good wide track on the ground to the right side of the wall bordering the conifers. There may be a bull in this field. Continue alongside the wall and where it ends, as unhappily it does, go straight on over the open grass to a gate out on to a minor road about 100 yards on.

Turn right here and walk uphill to a road junction. Here is a sign pointing to Rushend and Donkley Wood. This is the point where the alternative route mentioned above joins the footpath route. Turn towards Rushend and pass the farm and cross the Lairney Burn by the road bridge. The road now turns left and then right lower down. At the angle where it turns right leave it and descend beside the Lairney Burn to an awkward stile in the wall on the right. Over that cross the rather boggy section and go under the railway arch to the pasture beside the North Tyne. Follow the grassy ridge right past a wooden hut and recross the river by the parapeted bridge used at the beginning of the walk. Retrace the field path south to Hott.

Walk 15 — Elsdon

3 miles (5 km)

OS sheet 80, grid ref 936933

This is a short easy walk suitable for drowsy summer afternoons when the meadows are full of wild flowers, or for bracing winter weather when daylight hours are short.

The broad green of Elsdon is sparsely fringed by cottages and isolated in the centre of it is the church of St Cuthbert among its trees and gravestones. The vicar's pele, a reminder of border feuds, overlooks the northern corner; the Bird in Bush inn, the western exit towards Otterburn. The so-called Mote Hills on the northern outskirts date from the Norman period and are the earthworks of a motte and bailey castle.

Park on the side of one of the several roads through and round the green.

Leave at the north-east end on the B6341, Rothbury road, crossing the Elsdon Burn by the road bridge. Immediately afterwards leave this road and go straight on between the barns and the house and past the village hall towards the eastern side of the Mote Hills along the walled lane, part grass, part surfaced, to the gate beside High Mote Farm.

In the field ahead turn diagonally right and uphill, not keeping to the track alongside the wall but making over to the gates some hundred yards to the right of the old quarry workings at the upper end. There are two wide gates and a wicket here. The left-hand wide gate has a National Park footpath sign affixed to its upper side. Through this follow the sunken, somewhat overgrown lane to the left of the dyke and spaced hawthorn trees to the corner of a surfaced open road beyond the next gate.

Turn left on this road, cross the cattle grid and continue along through the meadows. Hudspeth, the farm and cottages on the narrow watershed between the Park and Landshot Burns, is the northern limit of this short walk but open heather moors lie further up the little ridge for those who wish to explore the foothills of the Simonsides.

For the present walk continue through the gate at Hudspeth and cross the Landshot Burn by the tiny footbridge beyond the poultry sheds. Climb the steep bank and continue across the pasture to the far side and uphill a little aiming towards the gate. (In misty conditions note that the compass bearing is 130 degrees from the bank top

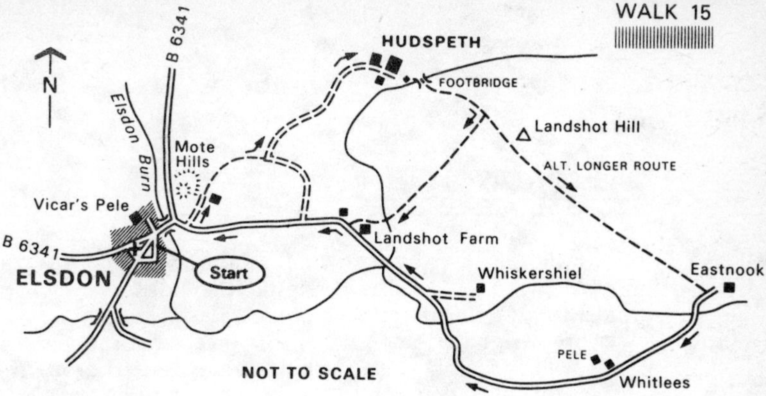

above the bridge.) Through the metal gate the right of way crosses the next enclosure directly towards a metal gate in the far wall.

For another longer walk continue through this gate and contour on in the same direction until eventually joining the road at Eastnook on the Whiskershiel Burn. Turn right on the road and follow it back past Whitlees with its small pele tower; go on past the turn-off to Todholes, by-passing the road end to Whiskershiel and on to Landshot Farm.

For the original short walk leave the hillside in the second field beyond Hudspeth when directly in line with Landshot Farm and on the near side of the descending wall, not going through the metal gate. Walk downhill with the wall on the left, going through an iron field-gate in a cross wall and crossing the Landshot Burn at the bottom at any convenient point near the little broken footbridge. It is merely a step over the burn. Climb up to the left side of Landshot Farm and go through the gate in the wall to join the open road beyond.

Turn right and follow the road past the second house and straight on at the road junction ignoring the turn-off to Hudspeth. Cross the cattle grid into the last enclosure before Elsdon. The village lies ahead and the Mote Hills are to the right. The road returns to the B6341 at the point of departure beside the village hall.

Walk 16 Rothbury Carriage Ways

5 miles (8 km)

OS sheet 81, grid ref 057015

This is an easy walk centred on the town of Rothbury. The 'terraces' are carriage driveways at various levels on the hillsides north of Rothbury and although the area is part of the Cragside Estate several of the terraces are designated as rights of way on the definitive map.

Rothbury is well provided with parking spaces. Apart from the wide main street through the town there is a large park on the south side of the Coquet to the west of the road bridge, and another more picturesquely situated on the north bank above the river and below the main Rothbury to Thropton road, just beyond the western limits of the town.

The walk leaves the main street of Rothbury from the corner of the Queen's Head Hotel and up Brewery Lane. Where the lane turns right uphill use the footpath up the steps indicated by the notice and follow the direction of the road up to the next corner. Cross here and walk in front of the gabled, half-timbered estate cottages, round the far side and straight up to the footpath where the signpost proclaims 'Blue House $\frac{3}{4}$, Alnwick Road $\frac{3}{4}$'. Not far up is a kissing gate, from which the path climbs diagonally across several fields said to have retained their elongated shape from the medieval method of strip cultivation. The final section of the path to the Hillside Road goes straight up and is stepped.

At this road turn right and continue past the end of the houses and on to where it is redesignated as a footpath only. Shortly beyond the beech wood there is a stile on the wall and a kissing gate into the field up on the left. Walk diagonally up the fields above Addycombe Farm, cross the estate road and go downhill through the trees to the Alnwick road.

All around now is the well wooded Cragside Estate, created towards the end of the last century by the first Lord Armstrong. Turn left along the road over the Debdon Burn bridge and up the hill past various estate cottages to the first turning on the left about a quarter of a mile up from the bridge. This is the forest road to Debdon. Follow it to the end of the trees and out over the open moor, ignoring the tracks off to the right and descending to cross the Debdon Burn again. Continue up to Primrose Cottage. Opposite is a gate to a farm road and a public bridleway sign to Crocky's Heugh. Follow this delightful

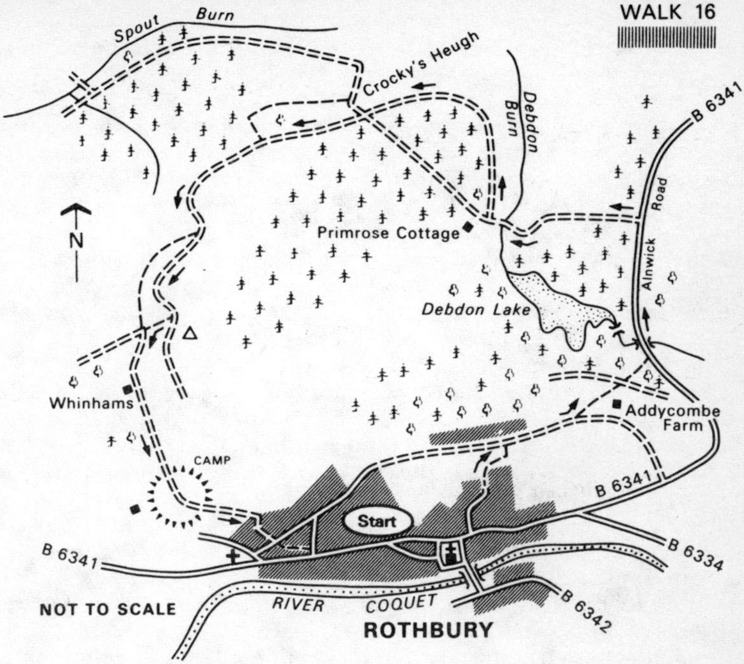

track round the edge of the woods above the upper valley of the Debdon Burn. Debdon Farm, backed by a long plantation, stands at the head of the little valley in the middle distance. Keep on the main track, curving round the trees on the edge of the moor and ignoring tracks leading off towards the farm. The main track curves back to the road with a gate beside another signpost pointing back to Primrose Cottage.

There is a choice of routes from here. The easiest and most sensible for those in shoes is that straight across signposted to Thropton and Rothbury. On a clear day better views are available from the footpath, shown on the map but invisible on the ground, which makes a loop round to the north along the rough heather and rock outcrops on the northern rim of the hill. To reach this go through the gate right and up to the highest part of the road just before it descends steeply to the valley of the Spout Burn. Leave the road and follow the rim of the escarpment using whatever sheep tracks may be available or ploughing through the heather and along the rock slabs. It is not difficult in boots. The views over Long and Coe Crags to the farther hills of mid Northumberland and the Cheviots in the northwest make it worthwhile. Eventually the right of way approaches a wall enclosing a conifer plantation and joins a path which comes up from the road below on the right. (This path is not shown on maps.) Turn left, i.e. south, and follow this narrow thread of a path to a little gate leading out on to the top 'terrace', the road which those following the easier route would use all the way from the Crocky's Heugh crossroads.

Now turn right and continue for about a half mile on the carriage way round the top of the hill until the land falling away on the right is sloping off towards the south and the main Coquet valley. The way curves in a wide loop to the left and then right again. Just on the far side of the loop a clear side track goes off to the right and leads gradually down towards a wall. Turn left, not through the gap in the wall, which is the way to Thropton, but keeping to the good track above the wall. Now keep to this track. It goes over the brow of a rise and downhill rejoining a wall bordering green fields. The land on the left is still open moor.

Pass the garden and house of Whinhams (Braeside on the O.S. map), and descend through tall pines and scattered silver birch. Below the trees the land rises slightly and heather and bracken give way to grass. This domed area is the site of an Ancient British camp. The ramparts and ditches are quite clear and the track goes over the top. The farm on the south west perimeter of the fort is Gimmer Knowe.

Descend to the wide gate and through that follow the road in a hairpin bend until it joins another road at a T-junction. Cross straight over and follow the narrow footpath via the stone stile and between the gardens of new houses. At the next road turn left and up a little to rejoin the path leading down to the main road opposite the County Holiday Hotel. The town centre is now to the left and the western car park to the right.

Walk 17 Thropton and Cartington

5½ miles (9 km)

OS sheet 81, grid ref 027023

Thropton is just under two miles west of Rothbury along the Coquet valley. It has a wide main street with some parking spaces. This walk, through fields, woods and moorland, is all on the north side of the village.

Begin on the east side of the bridge which carries the main road, the B6341, over the Wreigh Burn. This is in the dip below the Cross Keys. There is a little gap in the wall and a few steps leading down to the burn side. Walk upstream close to the burn, through a kissing gate and on to cross a footbridge over a side stream. The hinged barrier posts must be lifted to allow passage. Please replace them carefully. Continue along the Wreigh Burn, past its confluence with the Back Burn and on to the road at Snitter Bridge.

Turn left and follow the road up to Snitter Village, past Ladybank Cottage. Turn off right opposite the telephone kiosk and at the eastern limit of the hamlet, opposite the road sign bearing its name, go over the stile in the wall and walk north along the field edge to the far end behind the barns, where there is a gate on the left. Through this turn north again along a rough lane and on to what is usually an arable field, often very muddy. Keep up the left side close to the hawthorn hedge. At the upper end go through the wide gate and turn at right angles towards the south end of a little wood, a hawthorn hedge on the right.

There is a wicket gate into the wood. Turn immediately left and keep to the side of the wood for almost a hundred yards, then curve round to the right to the fine new footbridge over the Back Burn. This curve in the path avoids the rather boggy stretch south of the bridge. Now walk straight on, east, to the edge of the wood and on via the stile across to the far side of the field. Turn left here and walk up the edge of this field alongside trees and a wire mesh fence. This is not easy if the field is planted as tree branches impede progress. A few yards beyond the point where the field comes to the corner of a minor road, is a gate leading on to the road. Follow the road to Whittle Farm which has a most imposing but purely decorative wall on the east gable; a folly with arched 'windows', backed by a steeply pitched roof.

Walk right, i.e. east along the farm lane to the end of the first field;

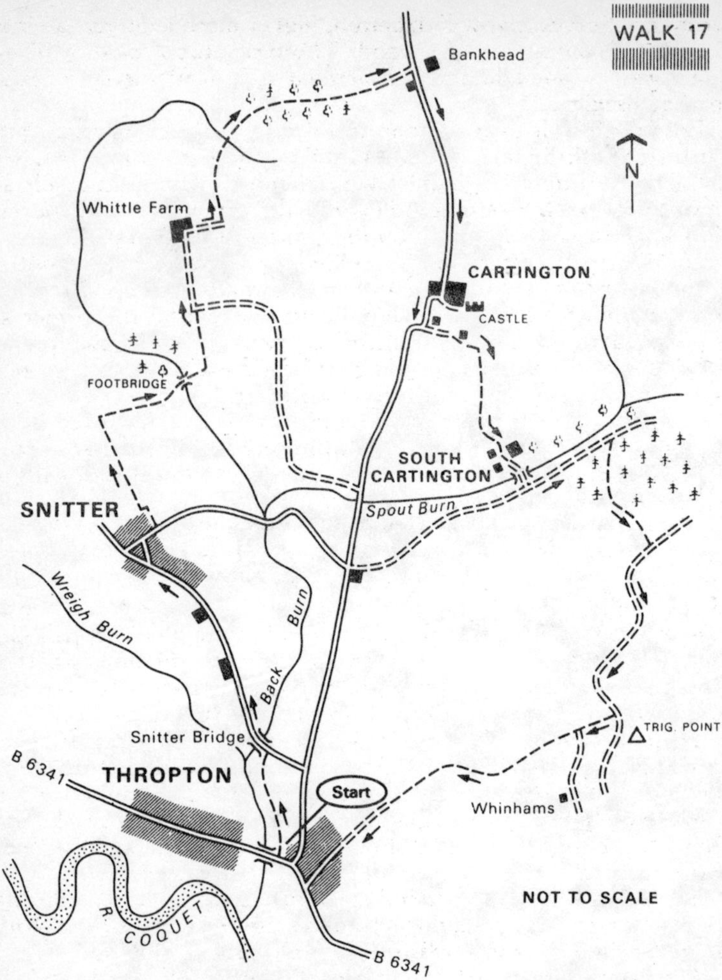

then turn through the second of the five gates on the far side of a ditch and walk north between a new wire fence and a line of tall mixed deciduous trees. Keep on past the fenced-in section into the open field and continue alongside the fence to a gate on the right which leads into the end of a long open woodland. There is a paling making a type of simple stile beside this gate.

Walk eastwards now, along the length of this wood as far as a barrier formed by a low embankment topped by a fence. A gate at the north-east corner leads out on to a farm track beside the wood. This provides a sensible diversion to the right of way as at present shown on the

Ordnance Survey maps. Further on, higher mesh fences make it impossible to continue in the wood. The farm track passes a disused quarry and a lime kiln and is concreted as it nears the cottages and road at Bankhead.

It is not possible to avoid a stretch of road walking from Bankhead. Turn right off the farm track and follow the road south for ¾ mile uphill to Cartington, a hamlet with a ruined castle and a splendid view down to the Coquet Valley and the Simonside Hills beyond. Notice the carved lion's head on the corner of Nunnery Cottage wall on the right. The castle is hidden behind the farm on the left. Continue to the last house at the corner where the road turns off sharp right and downhill towards the valley. Leave the road at the corner and turn left along the lane in front of the house following the footpath sign to South Cartington. Just before the garden of the cottage at the end of this lane is a footpath sign on the right.

Cartington Castle can be seen on the left. It was destroyed during the Civil Wars but the ruin was 'improved' during the last century, to make it more picturesque, by piercing the old tower wall with traceried windows.

Walk round the upper side of the field beside the edge of the garden to the gate with the yellow footpath sign and through this turn right and follow the field edges down to the valley of the Spout Burn. The lower end of the second field has a staggered corner and the path turns left and then right to the tiny hamlet of South Cartington. The right of way goes through between the line of cottages and the house and then bears slightly left to descend to the stone bridge over the Spout Burn and up to the T-junction.

Turn left and go up the red grit road, part of the Cragside Estate carriage ways. Pass the little waterworks building and ignore the first wide gate into the plantings on the right. Continue up between the beech wood and the spruce plantation to the second gate on the right. This is near the upper limit of the beech wood and is signposted to 'Rothbury 1¾'.

Now follow the forest road indicated by this sign. Keep on the main route joining a higher road which curves right. At cross-tracks further up go straight over towards the open moor.

A broken wall rims the forest here. Follow it left a little and then leave the forest road and keep to this wall as it climbs along the edge of the plantation. The right of way is just inside the forest and the wall is on the right hand. At the angle in the wall at the upper edge of the trees there is an old stone stile leading out on to the heather moor. Climb over and go straight on uphill over the heather to the wide level carriage-way on the plateau.

Now turn right and follow this easy grass and gravel track round the first big curve and on to the second until the full range of the Simonsides comes into view on the far banks of the Coquet and in the immediate foreground a trig. point is visible on the moor ridge ahead.

Look down now to the wall on the moor edge to the right for a gate leading to a lane through the pastures below. Cross the moor on any convenient sheep track to this gate. It lies due west of the trig. point.

Go through it and follow the grass lane down between a wall and a line of trees. Lower down the lane zig-zags in wide angles first right and then left but it is easy to follow. It descends to cottages and then the main Rothbury road, the B6341, again at the east end of Thropton. Turn right and along to the village.

Walk 18 — Alwinton via Wholehope and Kidlandlee

7 miles (11 km)

OS sheet 80, grid ref 921064

Alwinton is a small village, the last of size enough to be so called, along the upper Coquet valley. It is a very old settlement and has a church, a little distance from the village, dating back to the Norman period. The Rose and Thistle has been enlarged and modernised and, though lacking the atmosphere of the old inn, is still most welcome and welcoming, especially on a raw day with icy mist on the hills. There is also a large car park on the north side of the main street. Please use this for parking and not the pleasant village green.

The walk follows Clennel Street for about three miles. It is an old drove road which leaves the village from the north-east end of the green and is a walled lane for the first section. It climbs quite soon between the fields and out on to the open high pasture of Castle Hills, the first knob to the left of the track and the site of an Ancient British camp. This vantage point is on the spur between the Alwin Burn and the Hosedon Burn, both with steep-sided narrow valleys and domed hills between.

Clennel Street Cottage, now unoccupied, stands lonely to the right; the Clennel Street is a clear wide track climbing steadily up the spur and generally a little to the east of the summit but unmistakable on the ground. Where the spur narrows the track looks down to the deep Hosedon valley where it turns sharp south. The upper valley cuts back west and the stream is called the Alwinton Burn in its upper reaches.

Over the next rise the forestry of the upper Alwin points its dark fingers into the hills; the Street curves round Uplaw Knowe and Hare Sheds above Kidlandlee Dean which, hidden now by trees, falls steeply down ahead and to the right. The dilapidated remnant of the once cheerful Youth Hostel of Wholehope has still enough substance to provide a landmark, but there are plans to dismantle it and a commemorative stone will mark the site.

Beyond Wholehope, Clennel Street goes into the forest. The old right-of-way from Wholehope to Kidlandlee is so rough and difficult now that most walkers use the forest road. This is shown on the one-inch and the new 1:50000 Ordnance Survey sheets but not on the 1:25000 First Series. Soon after entering the forest, leave Clennel Street and turn off right on the road above the Kidlandlee Dean.

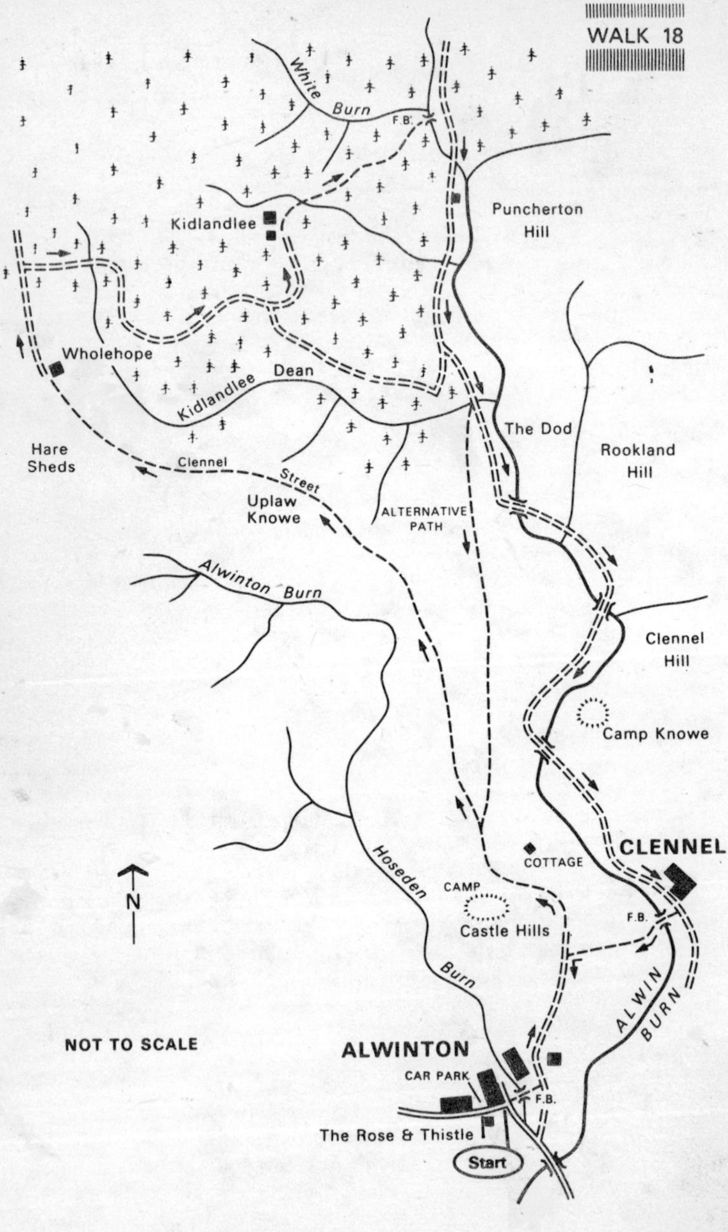
WALK 18
White Burn
F.B.
Puncherton Hill
Kidlandlee
Wholehope
Kidlandlee Dean
Hare Sheds
Clennel Street
Uplaw Knowe
The Dod
Rookland Hill
ALTERNATIVE PATH
Alwinton Burn
Clennel Hill
Camp Knowe
CLENNEL
COTTAGE
CAMP
Castle Hills
Hoseden Burn
F.B.
ALWIN BURN
N
NOT TO SCALE
ALWINTON
CAR PARK
F.B.
The Rose & Thistle
Start

It is a very pleasant route. The trees are still small and there are fine views over the Dean.

At the road junction turn left and follow the uphill road to Kidlandlee. Once a sizable hamlet with a school and a fair-sized mansion, used as a shooting lodge, it has now only one or two occupied cottages.

Go down via the small gate into the pasture below the cottages and below the grounds of the former mansion, curving round the upper edge and down by the far wall to the little kissing gate well down the bank. This leads into new plantings. Turn right and follow the narrow little path up on to the spur between the Alwin and the White Burn. Now keep to the edge of the very steep little ridge, descending on the north side to the footbridge over the White Burn at the bottom.

Cross to the Alwin valley road and follow it downstream to Clennel, crossing and recrossing the Alwin several times on the flat road bridges. At Clennel there is a good footbridge over the Alwin near the entrance gates to the Hall. The mansion was added to an early medieval pele tower. Go over the footbridge and up the bank to the little gate in the fence above. Through this, turn left and walk a few yards to the grassy ridge which marks the line of the old field boundary and walk on this west to the field gate and then along the edge of the next field back to Clennel Street near the starting point. Turn left and follow the lane down to Alwinton.

Walk 19 — The Street, Windy Gyle and Trows

8 miles (13 km)

OS sheet 80, grid ref 859115

This walk is over some of the more remote parts of the Cheviots and should not be undertaken without a map and a compass. It goes up to 2,000 feet.

Drive right up the Coquet valley and park about six miles beyond Alwinton at the foot of the Rowhope Burn. There are broad grass spaces here.

After leaving the car, walk westward along the road to the foot of the Rowhope valley where a side road turns off for the farms of Rowhope, Trows and Usway Ford. Cross the Rowhope Burn by the road bridge and go through the gate leading to the 'Street'. This is an old drove road from the Coquet valley to Hownam over the Border on the Scottish side. It is clearly to be seen rising up the ridge west of the Rowhope Burn.

Climb up the good clear track. It keeps to the ridge of the spur. About 100 yards up, there is a notice directing Army vehicles. It is not intended for the rambler. Keep straight on up the hill with a fence on the left. The long valley of the Rowhope Burn is down below on the right and, as the first few miles up to Windy Gyle are routed to go right round the head of this valley, it is as well to keep it in view most of the time although there should be no difficulty finding the way. It is a good broad track if somewhat boggy in places. At a stagger in the fence the track goes through to the other side. Where it branches it is better to keep to the eastern side, so keeping the Rowhope valley in view, but the branches converge higher up.

Up on Black Braes the track goes into a gulley and this provides some shelter. It is the only shelter for some time after this. Just before the Border fence the Street crosses the Pennine Way, now a well worn track on the ground. Follow the latter to the right and near the summit, left, go on up to Russell's Cairn on top of Windy Gyle.

The antiquity of this and other cairns on this ridge is uncertain but they are much older than the incident after which the main cairn is named; that is the murder of the Lord of the Marches, Sir Francis Russell, in 1549. It is difficult to visualise these quiet green hills as the backcloth for bitter feuds carried on for generations.

Cheviot and Hedgehope, the highest of the Cheviot Hills, fill the skyline to the north-east. On clear days the view is magnificent and

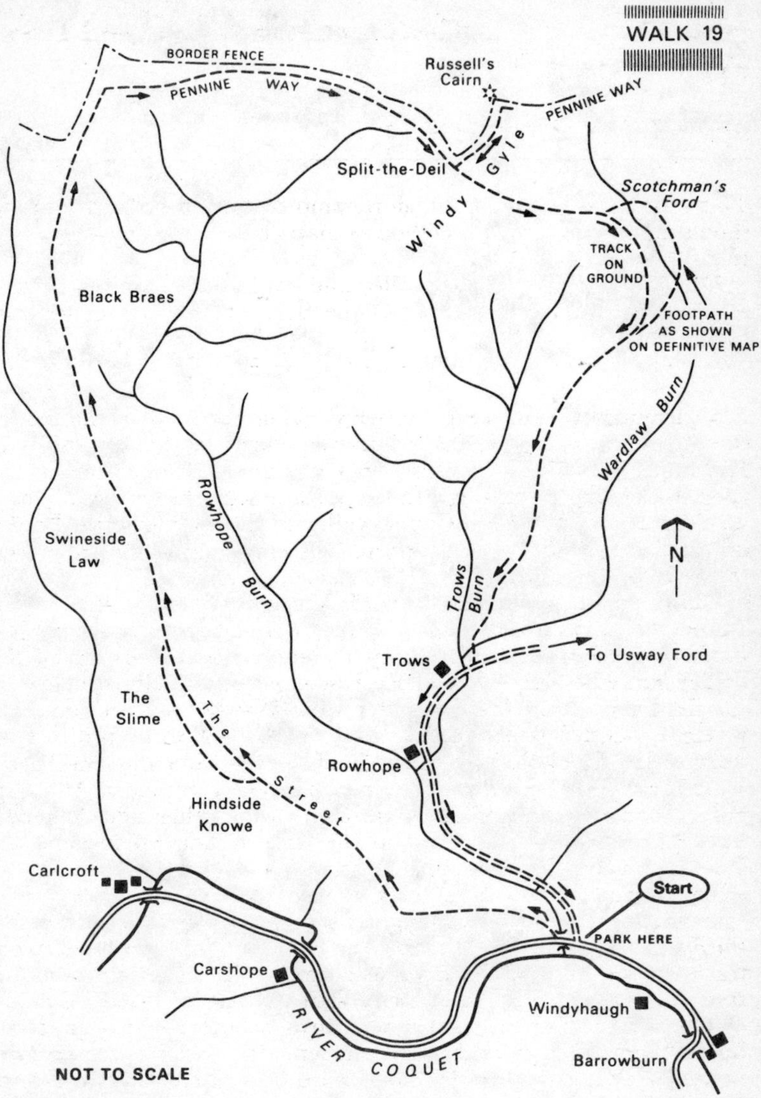
WALK 19
BORDER FENCE
PENNINE WAY
Russell's Cairn
PENNINE WAY
Split-the-Deil
Windy Gyle
Scotchman's Ford
TRACK ON GROUND
FOOTPATH AS SHOWN ON DEFINITIVE MAP
Black Braes
Wardlaw Burn
Rowhope Burn
Swineside Law
N
Trows Burn
Trows
To Usway Ford
The Slime
The Street
Rowhope
Hindside Knowe
Carlcroft
Start
PARK HERE
Carshope
Windyhaugh
RIVER COQUET
Barrowburn
NOT TO SCALE

worth the ascent from the last angle of fence, although these few hundred yards are to be retraced to continue the walk.

This angle of fence is on the south-west end of the Windy Gyle summit, lower than Russell's Cairn, and is known as 'Split-the-Deil'; the Devil in this instance being no doubt a pseudonym for an Englishman or a Scot in some foray.

The descent east, then south and south-west is clearly marked by a jeep track. It curves round as it approaches the upper valley of the Wardlaw Burn, which the right of way, as shown on Ordnance Survey maps, crosses at Scotchman's Ford to recross a little lower down. The jeep track keeps west of the burn and turns off gradually south-west on the spur between the Wardlaw and Trows Burns. In mist, if the track is lost, avoid crossing either burn and continue downhill on the rough grass slope to the farm road at Trows.

Turn right along this and follow it downstream beside the Trows Burn to Rowhope where it curves south-east alongside the Rowhope Burn and joins the main Coquet Road.

Walk 20 — The Harthope Valley and Broadstruther

7 miles (11 km)

OS sheet 75, grid ref 956226

This is a walk for those who like wide open spaces. There are few landmarks and it is wise to carry a compass. Apart from a little road walking it is all rough grass and heather with a few rocks and boulders here and there, and sheep.

Drive out from Wooler along Cheviot Street and continue to Middleton Hall. Turn right and drive up the very steep hill and past the two houses at Skirl Naked. Park on any suitable part of the grass verge between the Carey Burn bridge (the first road bridge) and the Hawsen Burn bridge just over two miles up the valley.

About a hundred yards east of the Hawsen Burn a Public Bridleway sign indicates the direction to Broadstruther and Wooler Common. Leave the road at this point and walk north-west and gradually uphill towards and across to the valley of the Hawsen Burn. Keeping fairly close to the burn follow it upstream on the east bank.

After about a quarter of a mile a much more definite track can be seen on the other side approaching from the south-west. This eventually crosses the burn and goes off uphill towards Broadstruther. Follow this track as it leads away from the burn and crosses the col between Broadhope Hill and Cold Law. A long wire fence is set at right-angles to the line of the path between the two hills and a gate close to a boundary stone allows passage through. From here the isolated ruin of Broadstruther Farm with its shelter belt of old trees, backed by the crags of Watch Hill beyond, provides a landmark in the otherwise wide featureless landscape. Aim towards it going below a corrugated iron shelter and contouring round in an arc to avoid the more difficult ground in the bottom of the Hazelly Burn valley which descends gradually from here towards the north-east. The path is now indistinct. There are two small streams on this side of the Hazelly Burn and these should be crossed fairly near their sources. The second of these is close to Broadstruther and on the far side of it is a new wire mesh fence with two strands of barbed wire along the top. A gate in this is approximately on the right of way but it is not necessary to go as far as Broadstruther. Turn right and follow the line of the fence towards the Hazelly Burn to a second gate. This is on another right of way from Broadstruther. Turn right again and cross the main burn by the ford.

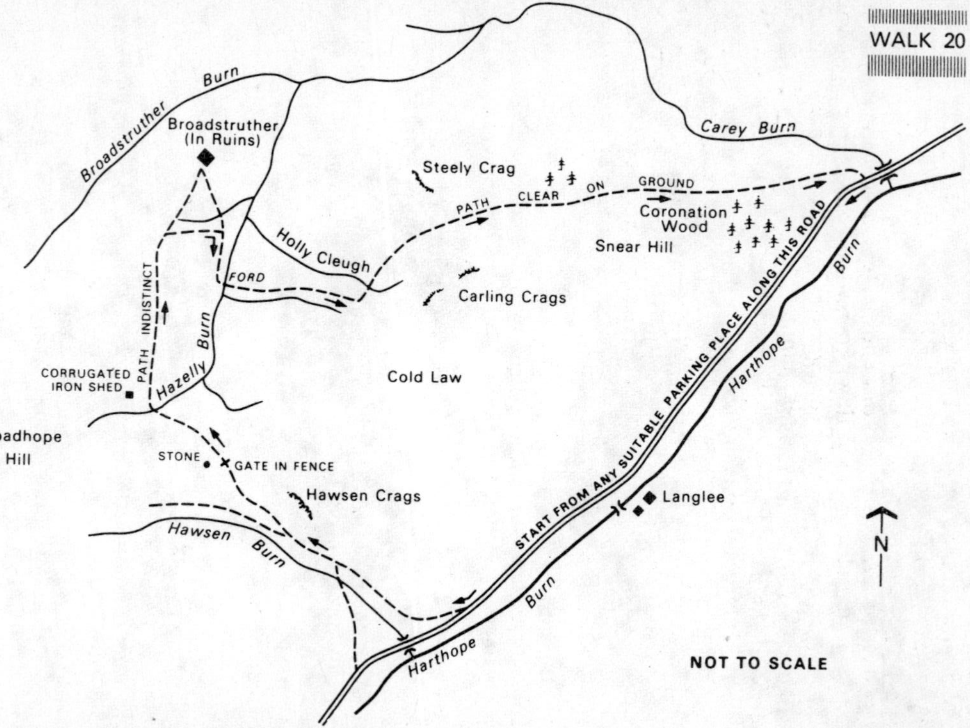
WALK 20
Broadstruther Burn
Broadstruther
(In Ruins)
Steely Crag
PATH CLEAR ON GROUND
Carey Burn
Coronation Wood
Snear Hill
Holly Cleugh
FORD
Carling Crags
PATH INDISTINCT
Hazelly Burn
CORRUGATED IRON SHED
Cold Law
START FROM ANY SUITABLE PARKING PLACE ALONG THIS ROAD
Harthope Burn
Broadhope Hill
STONE
GATE IN FENCE
Hawsen Crags
Langlee
Hawsen Burn
N
NOT TO SCALE

Through the gate on the far side go straight uphill. A new forestry track round the base of Steely Crag to the left now leads in the correct direction but there are better views from the top ahead. The path becomes clearer as it climbs and keeps just to the left of a long straight ditch. About 60 yards away, over to the left, is a more winding stream flowing down into the Hazelly Burn. Keep straight on past a small cairn over on the right, climbing to the brow of the hill where there is an isolated outcrop of rock called Carling Crag. The main hill over on the right is called Cold Law.

Over the brow the path descends to a wide gate in a wire fence and is easily followed back down towards the main Harthope valley. The white bungalow and cottages of Skirl Naked come into view shortly, and the far skyline is dominated by the knob of Ros Castle and the line of hills above Chillingham Park and Hepburn Wood south to Bewick Hill Fort.

Further down a small copse of tall thin windswept trees punctuates the bare hillside to the left and the path descends to the gate beside Coronation Plantation where it meets the new forestry track mentioned earlier as a possible alternative. Continue down to the valley road near the Carey Burn bridge and turn right and back along the road to the car.

Walk 21 — Gains Law and the Akeld Burn

7½ miles (12 km)

OS sheet 75, grid ref 976273

This is a walk over rough grass and open moor in the Cheviot area. Drive out from Wooler along Ramsay's Lane, which becomes the Commonburn House road, and park about half a mile out of Wooler on the open grass space beside the flat road bridge over the Humbleton Burn.

There is a public footpath sign on the north-west side of the burn near the bridge. Follow the direction indicated keeping close to the burn for about 50 yards, and then bear off left to ascend the hill on the broad green track through the bracken. Through the gate in the wall at the top ignore the paths off to the left and right and continue over the brow of Brown's Law where the track bears to the left and crosses rough ground in a westerly direction.

Shortly it comes alongside a broken stone wall and wire fence. Keep to this as far as the wicket gate at Drythropple, beyond which is the broad rough road up from the hamlet of Humbleton. Turn left along this for about 40 yards and then leave it to follow Coldberry Hill path off to the right. Keep roughly parallel to the line of trees climbing the hill to the right. Higher up, the track approaches a crumbling dry stone wall and keeps alongside it for a considerable stretch, leaving it to contour round the south side of Gains Law. The trig. point is visible for a time but disappears behind the shoulder on nearer approach.

On clear days the higher hills of the Cheviot range will be coming into view now. The regular cone to the south is Hedgehope; Cheviot itself to the south-west, with the long hump of Comb Fell between.

Below the wall on the north-west side of Gains Law is the deep little valley of Monday Cleugh and the site of an Ancient British camp on Harehope Hill on the far side. Many of these hills have evidence of early defensive settlements and Gains Law itself has indications of hut circles.

The track curves right, up to the wall and through a gate, and back in a hairpin round the head of the valley on the south side. This is one of three cleughs known collectively as the Trows. Follow the fence for a short distance until the track turns off quite distinctly to the south-west across the heather moor to a sharp angle in the wall that comes down from the summit of Black Law. Continue alongside

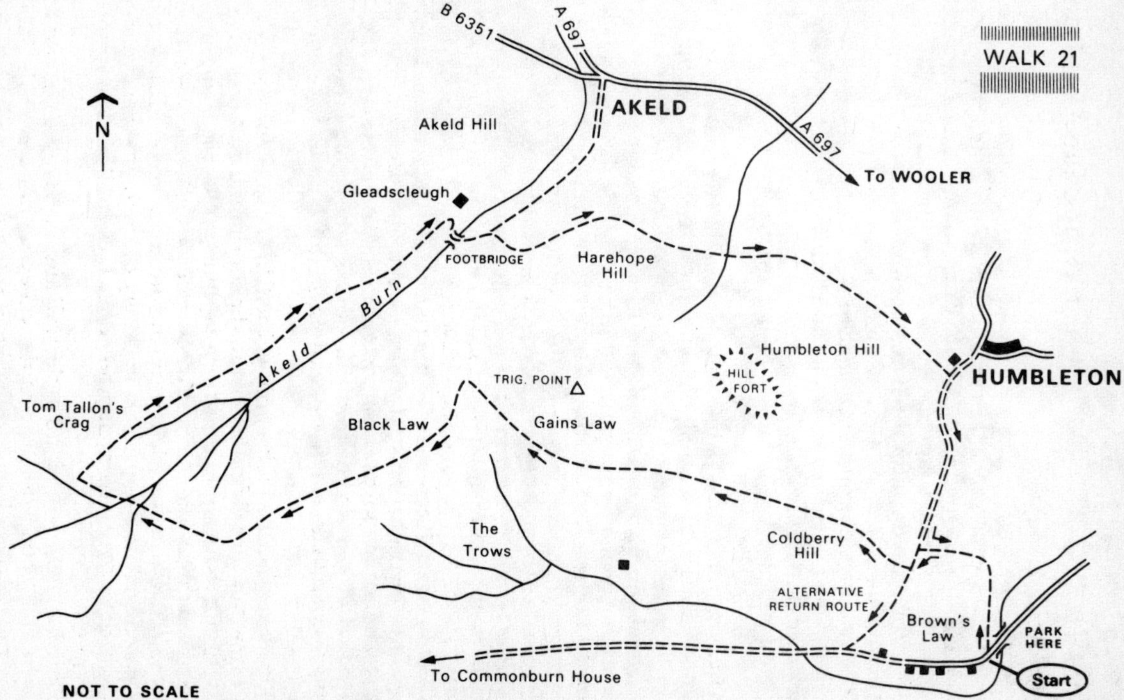
WALK 21
N
B 6351
A 697
AKELD
Akeld Hill
A 697
To WOOLER
Gleadscleugh
FOOTBRIDGE
Harehope Hill
Akeld Burn
Humbleton Hill
HILL FORT
HUMBLETON
TRIG. POINT
Tom Tallon's Crag
Black Law
Gains Law
The Trows
Coldberry Hill
ALTERNATIVE RETURN ROUTE
Brown's Law
PARK HERE
Start
To Commonburn House
NOT TO SCALE

the wall in a south-westerly direction until a stagger in the line of the wall carries the path through via a wide field gate to the north side. Now with the wall on the left go on to a wicket gate and out on to the descending wide basin forming the gathering grounds of the Akeld Burn. The valley dips away to the north-east round the foot of Black Law. Walk as far as the gate in the left-hand wall but do not go through. Turning away from this go down the slope aiming towards the confluence of the three little streams which meet to form the Akeld Burn. Isolated in all the vast expanse of open grassland and heath is a small triangular-shaped plantation. Aim for the right bank of the burn down to the right of this. There is no longer a clear path on the ground.

The return half of the walk is down the far side of the Akeld Burn where there is a clear path. Go up the far bank until you reach this track then turn right and follow it downstream, keeping well up above the stream bed. Ahead now are twin plantations; one on either side of the burn. The right-of-way descends the valley just below what is left of the north bank plantation. Most of the trees have been felled. A good green track goes all the way down to Gleadscleugh.

Just before the house turn down right and cross the burn by the bridge. Climb up the far bank and turn left towards a wall but do not go through by the gate. Climb the bank beside the wall and follow it round to the left at the top. At about the point where a long line of trees comes up to the wall on the left the path turns off right and curves round the side of Harehope Hill. Contour round to the wicket gate in the wall ahead and then down the steep pasture to a wicket gate in the opposite wall. Do not use the wide gate into the woodland below.

Humbleton Hill rises up on the far side of the valley. The little burn has come down from Monday Cleugh, mentioned earlier in the walk. The path continues round the north base of Humbleton Hill. Keep to the open land below the hill and to the right of the drainage ditch and small reservoir. Soon the roofs of Humbleton come into view and the rough road up from the hamlet is reached via a field gate near an old barn. Turn right up the road away from the hamlet and climb up to Drythropple near the beginning of the walk.

Return to base either by the same route as the beginning or continue over the saddle between Browns Law and Coldberry Hill by the main track to the road. Turn left on this and walk back to the car past Petersfield Cottage.

Walk 22 Hepburn Crag and Blawearie

7 miles (11 km)

OS sheet 75, grid ref 072248

This moorland walk should be undertaken on a clear day as the views are the main feature of it.

Park in Hepburn Wood Forestry car park or on the grass verge beside the road on top of the hill. The road crosses the moor between the A1 at North Charlton and the Alnwick to Chatton road. The car park is at the edge of Hepburn Woods just south of Chillingham Park and opposite Hepburn Tower, an old bastle house or small pele.

The line of the right of way from the car park is on the forest track to start with. It leaves this at the corner just inside the forest where the track turns right and the old right of way goes steeply up under the trees between two tiny streams and comes out on to the moor just under Hepburn Crag. An easier way up is to go out on to the motor road from the top corner of the car park and walk up past the cattle grid to the upper edge of the plantation and follow the way-marked path up on to the crag on the open moor. The summit is the site of Ancient British earthworks. It is a plateau-like circle surrounded by ramparts and a ditch, still quite evident among the heather and bracken. From it there are fine views over Chillingham Park and west to the Cheviots.

Cross straight over to the opposite side of the hill fort using the path made by the Forestry Commission. Keep on the summit ridge of the crags, walking south over the rough grass, bracken and heather above Hepburn Wood. There are rock outcrops here and there. Where the cleared track comes to a wicket gate and goes into the forest beside a fire-warning notice, leave the prepared path and continue along the hill top alongside the wire fence. A spot height of 267 metres (875 feet), shown on the Ordnance Survey map is indicated on the ground by a small cairn. Aim towards it. The track is much less evident now. Keep in the same general direction to the left of the forest fence and on the indeterminate rim of the escarpment.

Eventually the route approaches a fence descending from a pile of boulders marked as 'Tumuli' on the map. The gate through the fence is about 50 yards up from the trees. The southern end of Hepburn Woods is natural deciduous woodland. There are many sheltered, pleasant spots for lunch-breaks among the small trees and rock outcrops at the forest edge and in clear weather the views are

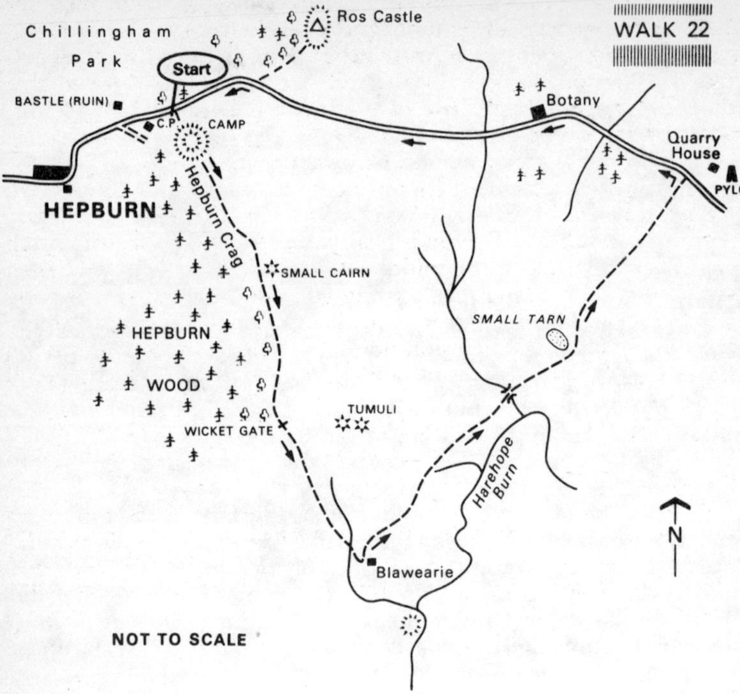

excellent. The broad valley below to the west is the Breamish-Till, which flows northward to the Tweed and Tilmouth. The broad-backed Cheviot and cone-shaped Hedgehope, descending to Dunmoor and Cunyan Crags, punctuate the skyline beyond.

After the wicket gate go straight on through the heather bearing slightly left. There are various sheep tracks. Keep roughly south over undulations until in sight of the ruin of Blawearie and its shelter belt of trees. Aim towards it making use of any convenient sheep runs. Look out for treacherous rabbit holes half-hidden in the heather.

Blawearie (to blow wearily) is well named; an eerie plăce but with signs of having been loved and cared for at some stage: trees planted for their blossom or fruit or shelter, carefully constructed stretches of wall to fill in gaps in the natural rock barrier on its eastern side.

The return route from Blawearie begins from the north-west corner of the old walled enclosure on the north side of the house. There is a single isolated sycamore here and the track leaves the corner diagonally across to the north-east and becomes a distinct track through bracken at first and then through heather. Here and there are tufts of rushes and care is needed where the track narrows across a boggy stretch. Look out for the white-topped television mast in the distance and aim in this general direction. Ignore a side track to Castle Crag.

Now the track widens and crosses the Harehope Burn by a flat cart-bridge. Further on is a gate in a wire fence and shortly after that a ditch across the track. A little care is needed here. The track disappears briefly but is clear enough shortly. It continues between a small hill on the left and some rock outcrop on the right. Over the next rise the track veers east somewhat to avoid a small lake shown on O.S. maps. It is now very much overgrown with rush, weed and sphagnum and not at all obvious from a distance. A poor little birch struggles for existence in the middle. The track curves east and then west round the far side of this, passing left of a sheltered spot among rock outcrops on the north side, and then turns north again roughly in the direction of the television mast. It is clear and green among the heather. The high hump of land to the left is Ros Castle, site of an Ancient British camp.

The track comes out to the road a little west of Quarry House where a radio pylon provides another landmark. Turn left along the road and return by it to the starting point.

The energetic may care to climb Ros Castle as an extra. In clear weather it is worth it. From the viewing platform on the summit seven castles may be seen, much of the coast and more of the Cheviots and perhaps even a glimpse of the wild white cattle in Chillingham Park down below.

Walk 23 Belford

10 miles (16 km)

OS sheet 75, grid ref 108339

Belford is on the A1 and easily accessible. There is some parking space in the centre in front of the Bluebell and some in the side roads.

Walk west along the B6349 Wooler road as far as the Belford Community Club and then north on the unclassified road. After about 100 yards notice the kissing gate on the left. This is the return point for the end of the walk. Continue on the road. The castellated building in the field on the left is on the site of the once moated 'Castrum de Beleford' and is now West Hall Farm. To the right are the inland-facing cliffs typical of this coastal area.

Turn left at the barns, then right and north again before the last barn. Continue to Craggyhall Farm passing farm cottages and a brick bungalow with a very pretty garden, then through a red metal gate past lime kilns and along beside a dry stone wall backed by briers, hawthorn, gorse and broom. The road ends at pasture. Keep straight on and go into the wood ahead via the wicket gate. This is mixed woodland with tall Scots pine and beech. Thick bracken forms the undergrowth.

At the junction with the forest ride the path ahead is private. Turn left and follow the ride out on to the road and continue west until Swinhoe Farm comes into view. Now look for a path which turns north-east through a narrow strip of plantation to a gate at the far side. A flat concrete bridge crosses a tiny stream just before the gate. Walk up the right-hand side of the pasture and, through the gate at the top, turn right and follow the stream and line of telegraph poles. There is now a view of the coast ahead and presently, round the curve of the field, Holy Island. If sunny, the sparkling white beacon on Emmanuel Head may be seen.

There are three gates at the end of this field. Take that on the left and walk along the edge of the field beside the hawthorn hedge to the lane down to the Detchant road. Turn left at the road and follow it to Grey Mare Farm and continue between the farm and the row of cottages, straight on past the barn, the copse of tall deciduous trees and through the wide metal gate. Beyond this the track curves round by the wall. Follow it to the end of the first field and through the gate; then turn right away from the plantation and walk uphill with the long line of hawthorns on the right. Go out on to the open common

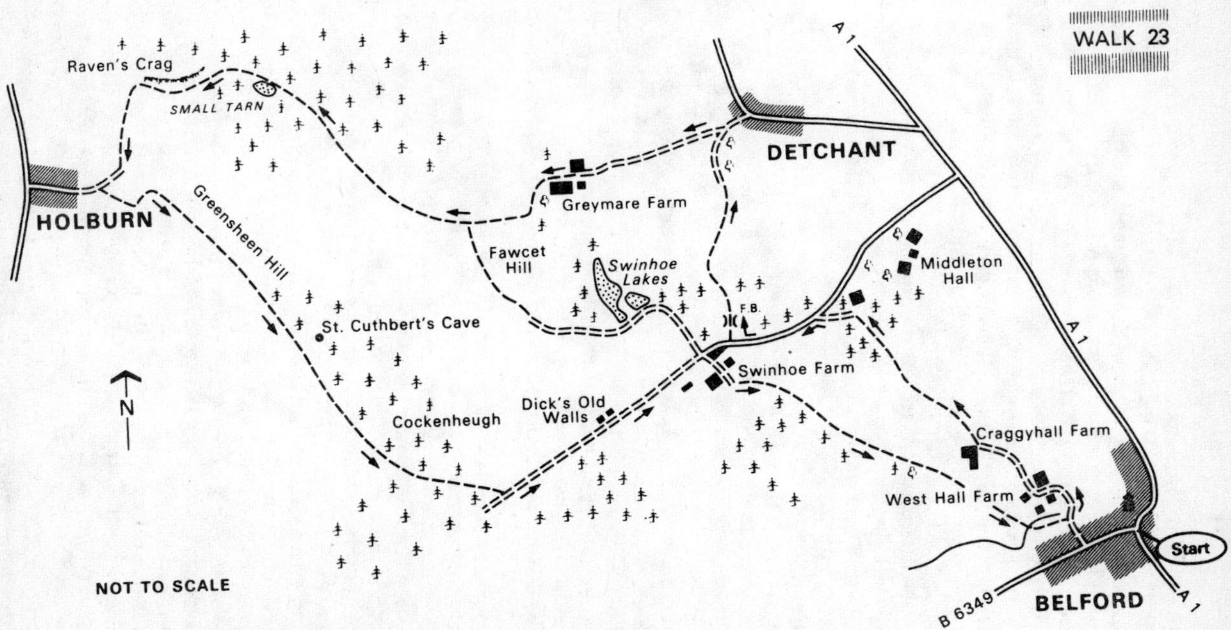
WALK 23
A 1
DETCHANT
Raven's Crag
SMALL TARN
HOLBURN
Greensheen Hill
Greymare Farm
Fawcet Hill
Swinhoe Lakes
F.B.
Middleton Hall
St. Cuthbert's Cave
Swinhoe Farm
N
Dick's Old Walls
Cockenheugh
Craggyhall Farm
West Hall Farm
Start
NOT TO SCALE
B 6349
BELFORD

at the top. There are wide views looking back towards the coast. Bamburgh Castle and the Farnes are now visible.

Just over the rise the track curves off to the right. Ignore the branch off to the left. It leads to old coal mine workings. The main track leads north to Kyloe Woods and enters the trees via a double gate. Heather lines the track and another inland-facing cliff rises up on the right. There are remains of more old mine workings in these woods and a small silted-up lake. It is advisable to keep to the track which is very easy to follow. Shortly after the reeds and rushes of the little lake, there is a gate leading to a younger section of the plantation. There is more heather and bracken here and a more open aspect. Ahead is Rabbit Hill and beyond that Raven Crag, a sandstone face with irregular bedding planes. The track curves round the foot of these, then turns south and through a gate, which is roughly the mid-point of the walk.

This is a lovely green track with bracken and gorse on the left and a stone wall on the right with views over to the Cheviots in the west. The little wood now being approached on the right conceals the track coming up from the hamlet of Holburn. Go on round the rim of the wood and down the lane to the edge of the moor, then turn left through a gate on to the moor and follow the boundary south, keeping fields on the right-hand side. There is a boggy stretch shortly, near to an angle in the fencing. It is easier to get along by the fence. After this the track is quite clear and keeps close to the fence all the way. The tall trees ahead are part of the plantings round St. Cuthbert's Cave, presumably one of the places where the Lindisfarne monks rested on their flight from the Danish invaders. The ground in front of the cave down to the right of way is consecrated as a burial place for members of the Leather family. The cave can be seen from the main track.

Continue south and then south-east along the perimeter of the plantation. There are open fields on the right. Great lumps of reddish sandstone outcrop in places on the left provide a miniature Arizona-type landscape. At the end of the trees the track goes along the edge of a green pasture becoming a wide, hard surfaced road through a tall narrow plantation, past the barn and one-time cottage of Dick's Old Walls and so down to Swinhoe Farm. Turn right at the crossroads here and go past the end of the line of cottages, past the granary and the big farmhouse and into the field. Go up the rise to the stile by the corner of the wood and continue along the edge of the wood at the top of the field. There are now views ahead towards the beginning of the walk. At Juniper Hill go to the left of the gorse-grown mound and on to the far corner where a farm road leads off to Craggyhall Farm. Ignore this, climb the stile in the wall and continue by the field edge over the little burn and on in the same direction. The footpath enters the south end of the enclosure of West Hall Farm and then via raised stones above the stream and along a little lonnen to the kissing gate noted at the beginning of the walk. Turn right and walk down the lane to Belford.

Walk 24 Bamburgh

5½ miles (9 km)

OS sheet 75, grid ref 183348

Bamburgh is one of the most attractive of the Northumbrian villages. The castle seems to grow out of its great rock to protect and shelter the cottages round the green.

This is a fairly simple walk; it does not go far afield, and there are no gradients to speak of.

There is a big public car park off the coast road on the south side of the village, and there are various parking places near the shore along the Wynding, the coastal cul-de-sac which justifies its name and winds over the dunes on the north side. Wherever the starting point, follow the Wynding north to its end near the golf house and coastguard station, passing en route the well-known and unmistakable Stag Rock.

If the tide is reasonably low use the path at the foot of the grassy slope beyond the coastguard station and then walk on the beach across little sheltered coves and round on the sands to Budle Bay; or follow one of various paths along the dunes below the golf course. Some of the more exposed dunes have been planted with marram grass to prevent erosion. The tide comes close up to the steep banks and the rocks fringing the coves are barnacled and decorated with bladder seaweed.

The mound with its small castle away off to the north is Lindisfarne. Oystercatchers and cormorants are among the birds along the sea's rim. Watch for the incoming tide, as pools tend to form behind the unwary. The Waren Burn flows into Budle Bay from the south-western corner and joins with Ross Low, coming from the north-west, to form the channel of Budle Water. At low tide the course of these burns can be seen in the otherwise flat sands.

Follow the curve of Budle Bay round almost to its south-west corner. The Cheviot Hills, Hedgehope and the Cheviot summit, mark the western skyline on clear days. The Bamburgh to Belford road, the B1342, approaches the edge of Budle Bay as it nears Waren Mill, the tall brick building beside the mouth of the Waren Burn. Come in towards the shore to meet this road. The steep bank side on the approach is thickly grown with sea-buckthorn. There is a gate near a nature conservancy notice board. Go out on to the road here and follow it to the right towards Waren Mill.

WALK 24

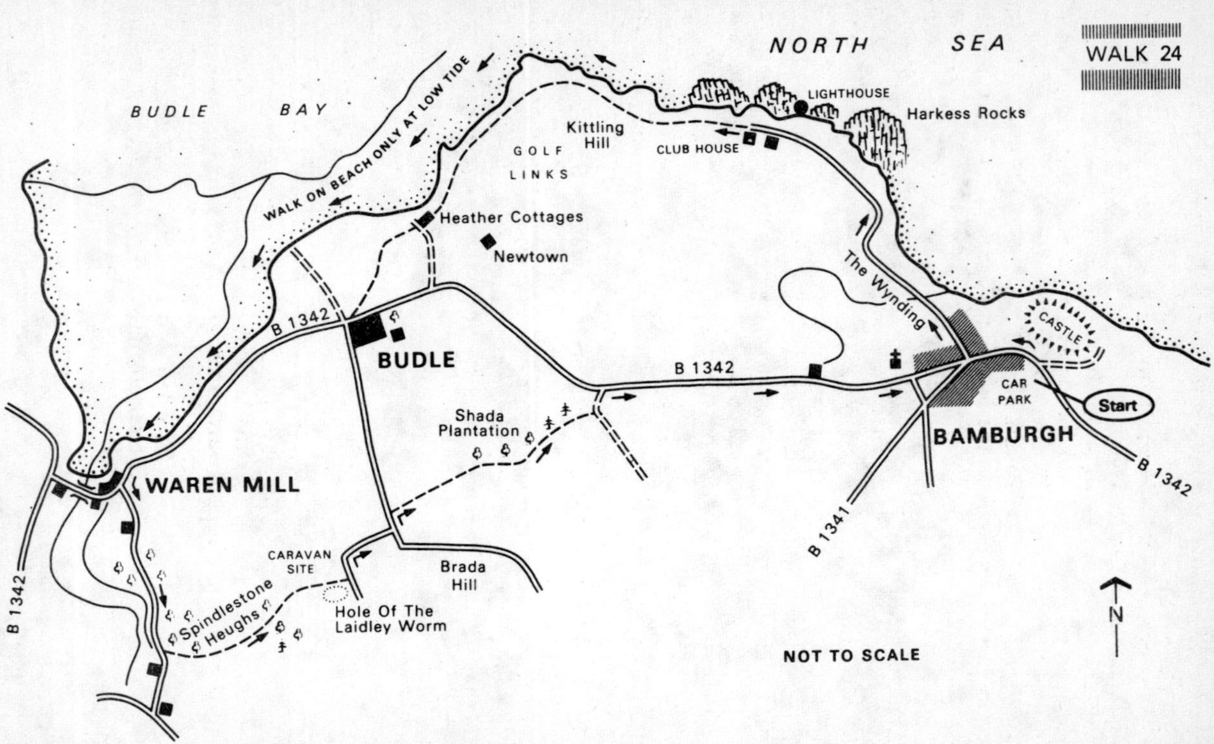

NOT TO SCALE

Although the walk turns off left just at the approach to the hamlet, it is worth adding the little extra to go on to Waren Mill if only to lean over the bridge and look at the burn as it flows into the sea over a small rock shelf.

To continue the walk return to the lane which leads off south opposite Waren Lea and along beside the wooded grounds of Waren House. Past this are fields on the right. Continue to where there are woods on each side and look for the wicket gate and the footpath sign on the left, indicating the direction to Drawkiln Hill.

Follow the path up the bank and on the edge of the wood, curving round further on towards the left as the edge of the wood curves. There is a lime kiln part way across the field on the right, facing an outcrop of limestone. The path goes via a gate in a tall hedge of trees into a green pasture and continues along beside the main woodland to a gap in an extension of it. There is an old wall alongside here and the tall crags of Spindlestone Heughs above the trees on the left. Go via another gate at the opposite side of the arm of woodland into a field. A caravan site is ahead. The right of way is along inside the edge of the site to a minor road but as there is a stile in the far corner of the field it is not necessary to go into the site.

The flat depression to the right of the hedge and below the miniature scarp slope was once a pond. It is shown as such on the 1 : 25000 map, and is the 'Hole of the Laidley Worm'. The ballad of the Laidley Worm is quoted in full in Tomlinson's famous guide.

At the minor road walk north to the junction by the entrance drive to the caravan site and walk east, i.e. right. The hill over to the right is Drawkiln. Bamburgh Castle comes into view from here.

At the junction with a more major road turn left and after about 20 yards climb the rough stone stile (do not go through the gate), following the direction of the footpath signpost to 'Galliheugh Bank, ¾'. The path runs along the right-hand edge of a field. Looking back in clear weather there is a fine view of The Cheviot and Hedgehope; to the north is Budle Bay and beyond that Ross Links and Holy Island; ahead, defying all comers across the North Sea, is the stronghold of Ida, King of Northumbria. The castle partially hides the Farnes from here.

At the end of this field climb the paling in the corner and continue towards Bamburgh to the right of a hawthorn hedge and then through a wicket gate to the right of Shada Plantation, climbing the little bank and then descending eastwards along the line of spaced Scots pine and gorse bushes. A stile across the field end leads out beside a footpath sign on to a minor road. Turn left and walk up to the road.

This is the B1342. The direct return to Bamburgh is east along this. It is less than a mile to the village centre.

Walk 25 — Craster and Dunstanburgh

4½ miles (7 km)

OS sheets 75 & 81, grid ref 256197

This walk can be added to the next one to make eight miles. Alternatively, if a short walk is required there are a number of short cuts.

Use the quarry car park just outside Craster and leave it from the west side of the outer section near the information centre, using the footpath at the foot of the wooded craggy rim of the quarry. This crosses a tiny burn into a field with a well used path clearly visible, leading away from Craster west across the back of Craster Tower grounds. (To shorten the walk use the road west towards the front of Craster Tower, or cross the road from the car park and use the footpath along the foot of the Heughs, the inland-facing cliffs on the north side, and then turn left to Dunstan Square Farm.)

The field path comes out on to the road near Craster Tower. Turn right and walk up to the crossroads, then right again along the avenue of beeches on the Craster road. Before reaching the old arched gatehouse pause at the cobbled entrance to the Tower. The house is mainly 18th-century but the Tower itself dates back to the 15th century. The late Sir John Craster was a well known naturalist and author and the family are said to have occupied the estate since the 13th century.

Continue along the road through the arch and then turn immediately left following the footpath sign to 'Dunstan ¼'. The path follows the field edge north. There are views of the sea and the inland-facing crags of columnar basalt known as the Heughs. At the north end of these are the jagged teeth of Dunstanburgh Castle ruins.

Turn right along the road through the hamlet of Dunstan, then left as it bends north in front of the telephone box. At the road junction continue north on the road signposted to Embleton. Pass Dunstan Hall, added to a 14th-century tower at various periods, then Proctor Stead and the caravan site. To the right now is an unclassified road to the farm of Dunstan Square. (This is a useful route for shortening the walk, especially in wet conditions as the longer route has one particularly muddy section. By using this route two other variations are possible from the farm. Either continue east to the Heughs and the footpath there, or turn north and follow the farm road to Dunstan Steads and thence over to the shore and south back to Craster by Dunstanburgh Castle.)

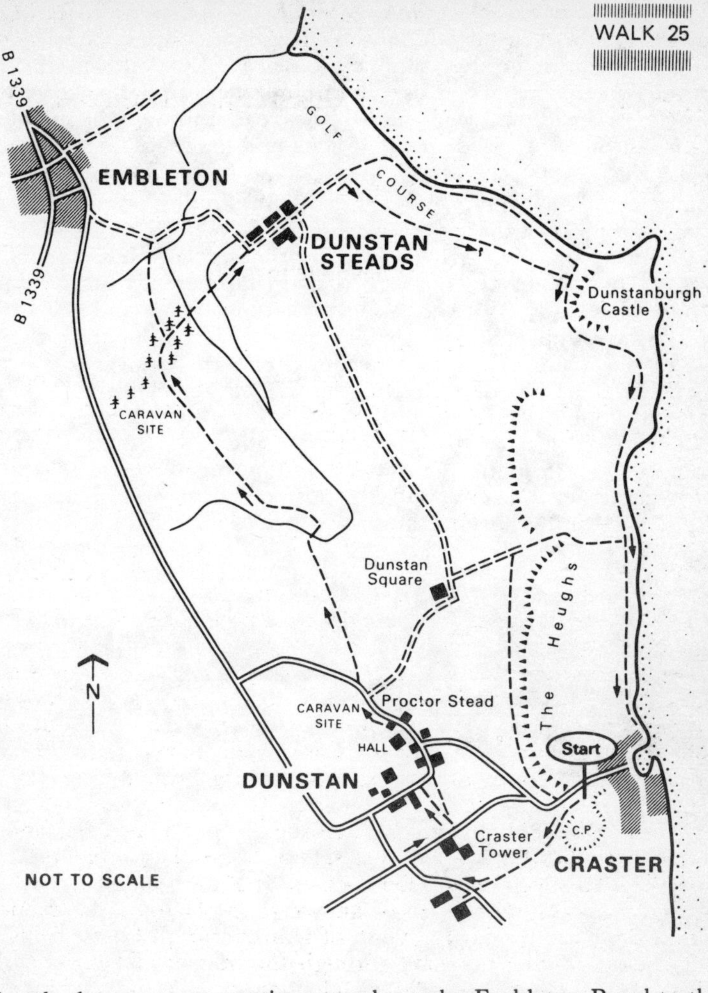

For the longer route continue north on the Embleton Road to the bend where the road turns left and a footpath sign to 'Embleton 1¾' indicates a good grass track straight on through arable fields.

The track continues to a gate near the plantation. Turn right through this and then left along the field edge and beside a little stream bed. Continue in this direction keeping to the left sides of the fields. Embleton is now clearly in sight. It appears to be sitting on top of a mound beyond the woods of the Embleton Burn. A caravan site now occupies the field to the left of the path, nearest to and south of a long plantation. There is a stile into the plantation and then a tiny footbridge over the little burn under the trees and a path which joins a good wide track running centrally down the length of the plantation. Follow it east down its whole length and through a gate into a field. Continue in the same direction up the field towards the chimneys of Dunstan Steads. Go through the gate signposted back to Proctor's Stead and walk down the road through the hamlet of Dunstan Steads towards the golf links and the sea.

To return to Craster either cross straight over the links to the sand dunes and follow the coast south to Dunstanburgh Castle, or keep to the path down the inland side of the links to the castle.

Dunstanburgh is a striking jagged ruin on a high basalt cliff, part of the Great Whinsill which crosses Northumberland and on part of which Hadrian's Wall was built. Cullernose Point and the various Heughs are all part of this volcanic system. The castle ruin is all original or 'pure' and dates back to the early 14th century. It was built by the Earl of Lancaster after the Battle of Bannockburn and altered later by John of Gaunt about 1380. It is open to the public.

The footpath skirts the inland-facing side of the great mound and continues south along the grassland adjacent to the rocks and the beach. Craster is just over a mile south of Dunstanburgh and has an attractive fishing harbour and some places of refreshment.

Walk 26 — Craster and Howick

3½ miles (5.5 km)

OS sheet 81, grid ref 256197

This walk can be lengthened into anything between five and eight miles if the Craster and Dunstanburgh walk, or parts of it, are added and one short section across a field omitted.

There is a spacious car park on the south side of the approach road to Craster in a vast disused quarry. There are two sections to the car park – a smaller outer section and a huge area inside the quarry.

Leave the park using the gate from the outer section on the coast side and walking on the track from here to Craster to avoid the road. Turn right between the first houses and walk south and then west along a good cart track at the back of a row of houses following a footpath sign to 'Howick 1¼'; walking back in the direction of the quarry for a short distance. Where yet another line of houses is built parallel to the coast go through a gate and turn left behind them, to walk southwards towards the grasslands adjacent to the shore.

From here there is a view back towards Craster harbour. If the tide is out the two groups of rocks known as Mickle Carr and Muckle Carr are visible outside the harbour.

Now keep to the coastal edge of the grass above the rocks and continue south towards the coastguard lookout station on Cullernose Point.

Cullernose Point is a magnificent cliff of basalt thrusting its bulk out to sea beyond the limestone slabs of the bay on its south side. Follow the top of the cliff inland to the gate and the footpath which leads through the thickets and approaches close to the road. Until recently it was necessary to use the road, but now a good path has been cut through the bushes, so it can be avoided. Continue down the coast to Sea House near Rumbling Kern.

There is a small sheltered haven just south of the house: an excellent spot for a rest or a picnic. The Rumbling Kern is so-called from the noise the sea makes as the tide rises into a chasm in the rocks on the seaward side of the haven. This can be visited by a miniature rock climb but a watchful eye should be kept on the rising tide. In stormy weather the breakers can be splendid but extra care is needed.

Turn inland by the narrow track along the field edge between Sea House and the haven, and a field width north of Howick Sea Houses, the line of terraced stone cottages just inland from Rumbling Kern.

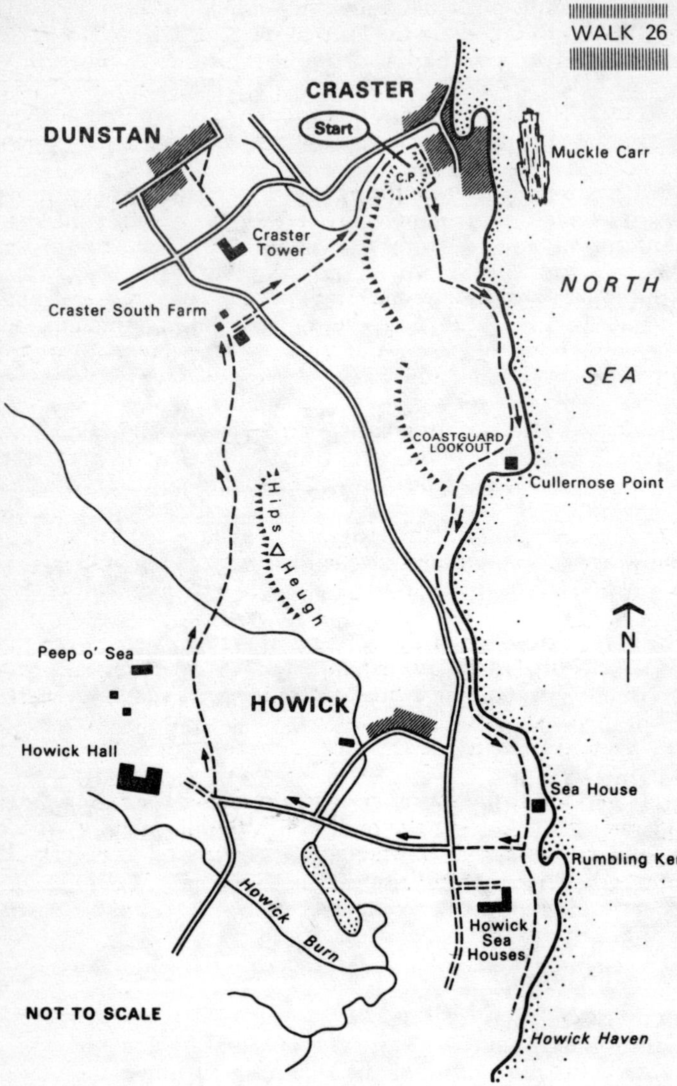

WALK 26
CRASTER
DUNSTAN
Start
C.P.
Muckle Carr
Craster Tower
NORTH
SEA
Craster South Farm
COASTGUARD LOOKOUT
Cullernose Point
Hips Heugh
N
Peep o' Sea
HOWICK
Howick Hall
Sea House
Rumbling Kern
Howick Burn
Howick Sea Houses
NOT TO SCALE
Howick Haven

This narrow path leads to a sharp angle in the coast road.

Follow the road inland to Howick Hall entrance gates. (The minor road through Howick hamlet joins this road not far from Howick Hall.) The grounds of the Hall are open daily.

The walk continues along the lane to the right of the entrance to the grounds, between the high wall and the pasture, coming into the latter by a field gate at the corner of the lane as it turns off to the left. Continue in the same general direction through another field gate and over a little burn, then bearing left round the edge of a ploughed field.

A farm, Peep o' Sea, inside the estate on the left looks out through a gap in the trees towards the coast. From the footpath the gables and chimneys of Howick hamlet are visible between the folds of land on the seaward side.

Go through the gate where the estate woodland ends, cross another tiny stream and, maintaining the same general direction, walk straight over a huge meadow towards the inland-facing, gorse-grown cliff edge of Hips Heugh and a ladder stile in the long wall on the near side.

Turn north in the flat grass area at the foot of Hips Heugh and, keeping roughly alongside the wall, pass two isolated sycamores and then curve gradually round to the right to the northern extremity of the rock outcrops and the angle in the far corner where the field boundaries meet. Go over the left-hand of the two ladder stiles here and, keeping the wall on the right-hand side, skirt the field edge in a gradual slight curve to the row of cottages and the Craster South Farm.

Turn right at the end of the cottages and go out on to the main road via the short lane. Craster South Farm is a picturesque group of farm buildings including a fine arched hemmel which can best be seen from the road. Turn left on the road if wishing to complete the longer walk and go up to the crossroads. (Now see the Craster – Dunstanburgh walk.)

To return directly to Craster cross straight over from the lane and through the gate following the path across the undulating meadow to the huge rock outcrops on the edge of the quarry car park. The path skirts these on the north side.

Walk 27 — Alnmouth and the Aln

7 miles (11 km)

OS sheet 81, grid ref 251107

There is interesting contrast in this route. Part of it is along or near the shore, part along the banks of the meandering Aln, and part through the old village of Lesbury. The upstream route along the Aln is a good wide track, easy to follow and full of interest, with abundant wild flowers and a variety of trees and birds. To return downstream on the opposite bank is for the more adventurous and certainly only for the boot-clad walker. There is a difficult stepping-stone crossing and the fields are planted or ploughed to the overgrown bank sides so that there is no clear track. It is, of course, passable for the determined and careful map reader. The easy south side of the Aln can be rewalked as an alternative or there is a farm lane available.

Parking space at Alnmouth is close to the beach and across the smaller golf course on the north side of the village. A charge is made in the summer season.

Walk south towards the village either along the sand or the dunes or the edge of the golf course. Keep to the seaward side of the village along Riverside Road, passing the ferry hut and the children's play park, to the corner where Garden Terrace turns off sharp right. Turn left here away from the road through a gap stile between the electricity sub-station and the wide field gate and follow the narrow, well-defined path to the riverside and round to the road bridge on the west side of Alnmouth. The river is tidal here and the sea comes close to the footpath at high tide.

There is a white kissing gate out to the end of the bridge. Cross the road, then the river, using the footbridge alongside the road bridge, and follow the road west along the pavement. Just past the entrance to the cricket club is a rather ornamental white gate into the field next to the school enclosure. Follow the field path north beside the hawthorn hedge for two fields and then along the back of new housing to join a by-road via a kissing gate quite close to a footbridge. Cross the Aln again and turn left along the path past the converted school building. Notice the crescent-shaped stone carving and the date, 1858. The crescent is one of the heraldic badges of the Percy family. Look for others through the village of Lesbury.

Turn left at the road and pass the church of St Mary and the post office and at the junction with the A1063 turn left again. Follow the

WALK 27

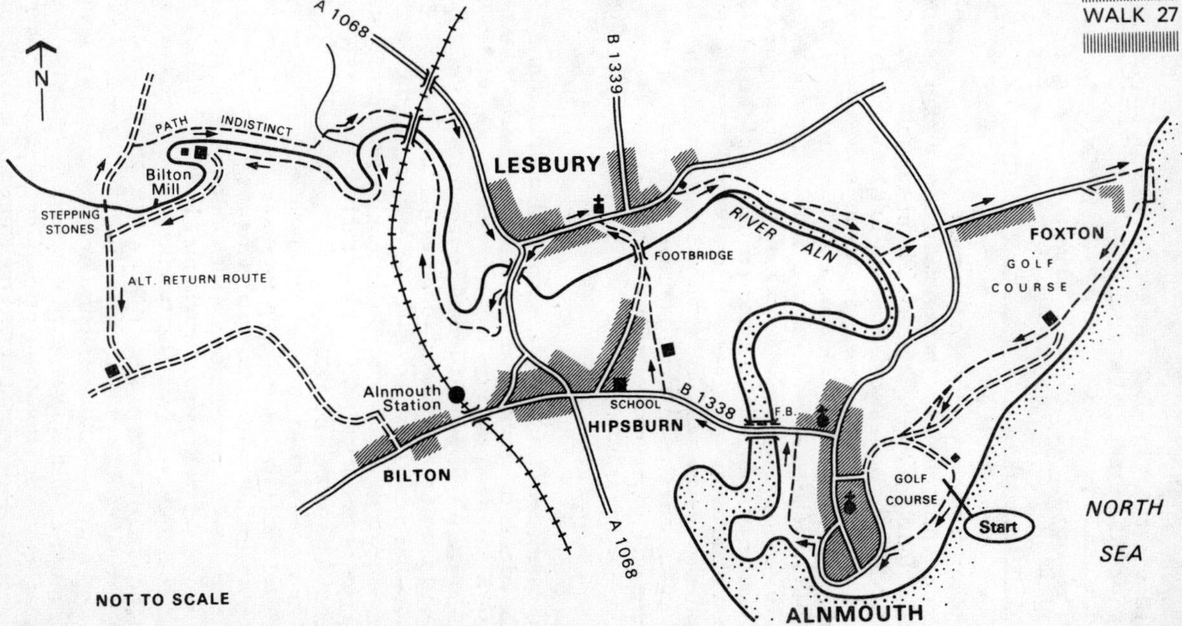
N
PATH
INDISTINCT
Bilton Mill
STEPPING STONES
ALT. RETURN ROUTE
A 1068
B 1339
LESBURY
FOOTBRIDGE
RIVER ALN
FOXTON
GOLF COURSE
Alnmouth Station
SCHOOL
B 1338
F.B.
HIPSBURN
BILTON
A 1068
GOLF COURSE
Start
NORTH SEA
ALNMOUTH
NOT TO SCALE

road towards Hipsburn, crossing the Aln and crossing the road past the decapitated arched wall of what was once a mill, to a footpath which runs parallel and close to the road.

Within sight of Hipsburn turn off this path through a kissing gate into the field on the right and follow the good double track round below a hedge. The track curves round towards the riverside further on. The embankment of the main London-Edinburgh railway is visible ahead. Pass a spring giving rise to a tiny burn and turn right over this towards the river, still on a clear wide track which now swings left below a steep bank and runs alongside the Aln through pasture and under a viaduct.

Beyond the arches the Aln curves south in a loop with the track coming almost back to the embankment, then right again in another loop towards the west, bringing to view parts of Alnwick and the scanners on top of the hill above Hulne Park. Along the banks ahead is the farm at Bilton Mill. Continue to this and round the far side of the house turning left between it and the barns to join the farm road on the south side. The river loops back on itself here and the farm road follows it west. About a quarter-mile from the farm, at cross-tracks, is the outer limit of the walk and the return is either over the so-called stepping-stones over the Aln, a few yards down to the right, or left along the farm road to Bilton and back by road to Alnmouth or Lesbury to rejoin the main walk described later.

It is possible to 'plodge' over the river for those prepared to take off their boots. The depth of the water varies according to recent precipitation but is not likely to be more than knee deep except after very heavy rain. The agile may manage the stepping stones. The track on the north side leads away from the river. Follow it for about 150 yards to the end of the first field on the right, where there is a gap. Turn into the end of this field and walk towards Bilton Mill, visible on the other side of the loop in the river. There is no clear track on the ground. Keep to the edge of this field and through a gap left at the elongated far end, then right and along the edge of the next two fields alongside the river. As the fields are probably in crop or ploughed, keep as close to the edge as possible and in single file.

In the next field where the river, concealed by trees, turns north at the far end, turn immediately left on entering it through the gap and walk at right-angles from the river and alongside the hedge. This is necessary to cross the little burn which flows east into the Aln. The only way to cross it is by the left-hand side of the field. The burn is hidden in undergrowth and trees but its course is clear enough. Turn right at the other side of it and go back towards the thick vegetation of the Aln banks. Now keeping to the extreme edge of the planted crop, follow the river bank round towards the viaduct again and go under the last of the arches on the north bank.

Through the wicket on the east side of the viaduct bear left and cross the rough grass and open wooded area diagonally to a stile in the wall on the right side of a tall beech and on to the road, the A1068.

Turn right and walk along the pavement for quarter of a mile to Lesbury. At the junction with the B1339 turn left in the direction of Longhoughton, Seahouses, etc., and return along the village past the school and church. Go straight past the next junction, leaving the B1339 and following where the sign indicates Boulmer and Foxton. At the corner ahead just past Holme House the right of way, surprisingly, goes through the garden of a bungalow between the gable end and the garage.

Go through the kissing gate at the back and come out into a field, and here is the river Aln again. Keep roughly parallel to it, later descending gradually to the far end where there is a gate just a few yards from the river. Two rights of way lead from here. The lower is likely to be less troublesome as there is much ploughing out and planting on the upper. The lower goes down to the riverside via a kissing gate along the bottom of a field in crop to a gate into open pasture. The upper route goes roughly straight ahead below a line of trees, across ploughed land, diagonally over a field in crop to a gate half-way up the steep bank, and into the same pasture. Using whichever track, climb to the top of the pasture by the line of telegraph poles and come out on to the road, through a gate to the right of the pole at the top.

Cross straight over to Foxton, along the private road (but public footpath), to Alnmouth Golf Club. The 1:50000 O.S. map shows footpaths leading either side of the club house to the beach. That on the left is clearer on the ground. It follows below the left edge of the car park and the side of the course down a little dip to the shore.

Turn right and walk along the beach beyond the end of the Foxton gardens and then there is a choice of return routes to Alnmouth. There are rocks and pebbles on the beach for a stretch but it is sandy further on. One path goes up to the top of the dunes just past the weather vane with the fox atop, and continues along the outside edge of the golf course, through a little gate, past the front of a fisherman's cottage to a bend in a grit road. Go right or left on this. The upper route continues between the upper and lower golf courses as a long green track with pleasant views. The left and lower route returns directly to base but has inferior views. The beach route needs no description but look for the car park between the dunes further on towards Alnmouth.

Walk 28 **Alnwick**

7 miles (11 km)

OS sheet 81, grid ref 185133

Although no longer the administrative centre of Northumberland and bypassed by the A1, Alnwick is still bustling enough in the holiday season and its castle is the seat of the Duke. On quiet days there is room to park near the town centre or in the market place but on market days look for parking space beyond the bus station, off the B6341, the Rothbury road.

Leave the B6341 opposite the bus station and go uphill a little, then up Tower Lane between flats on one side and stone terraced houses on the other. Turn right at the top and on to King Street, up that and right at the top again along Lisburn Street. At the end of the terrace or the opposite side turn left on to a path beside a bungalow and on past a school up on the right. Higher up the path ascends between walls, then opens out on the left over a little wooded dene and then a meadow, eventually coming out on to a curve in a road.

Go straight uphill on the road, passing new housing and the golf club entrance and on between trees, hedges and meadows to the corner at the entrance to Greensfield. Turn right and uphill here to the west side of Stoneyhill, then follow a walled cart track to the left of a modern house, between trees and along the edge of a field to the corner of a dirt road. Turn right here and go up to a hard-surfaced road.

Turn left along this to a junction at Intake Farm and then left again to follow the unclassified, but well-surfaced road towards Rugley. (The walk may be shortened considerably by going straight on from Intake to a point described later.) There are wide views from the Rugley road both over the valleys and fields to the south and back over the sea. It is a pleasant quiet country lane. Continue along it for two miles past the entrance to Hobberlaw, down over the footbridge beside the ford on the Rugley Burn, over the disused railway cutting, past the rhododendron-lined drive to Rugley and on to the T-junction.

Turn right and follow the road for three-quarters of a mile to the crossroads at Hadwin's Close. Turn right following the signpost direction to Alnwick. This is a pleasant breezy road with good views.

At the end of the first field from the crossroads go through the gate on the right and cross the second field diagonally, crossing an old

WALK 28

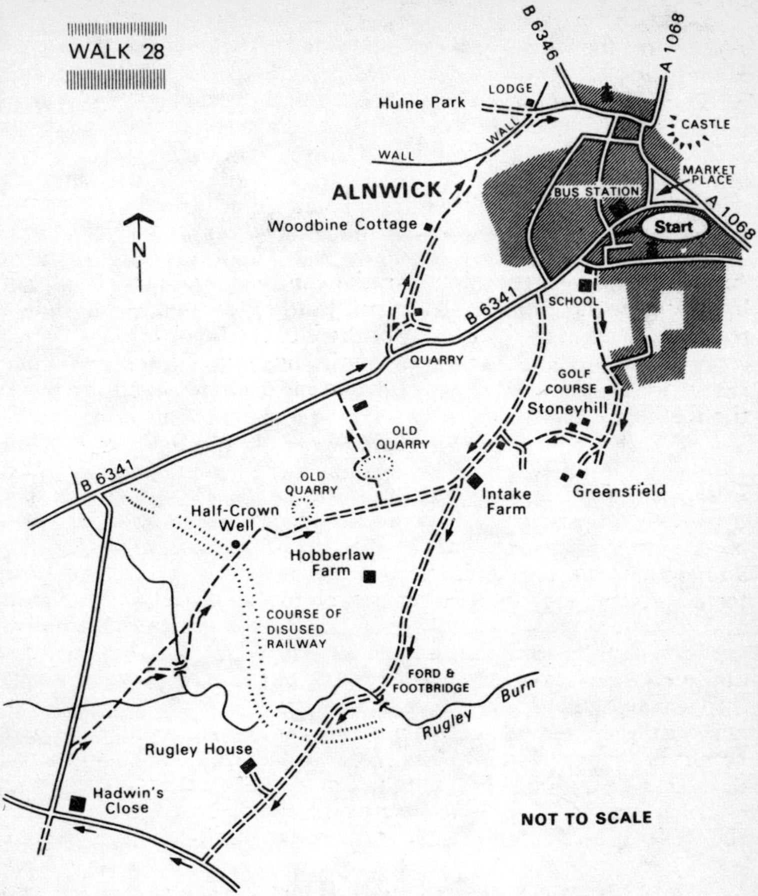

raised gorse- and hawthorn-grown track, and on towards the next boundary keeping about a third of the way down the field from the road. The line of the right of way leads to a broken stile beside a little burn, the Linn Letch. A footbridge is marked on the 2½ in map but there is no sign of it now. Step over the burn and continue to the Black Burn cart bridge, a little to the right of the two gates at the next field boundary. The cart bridge is slightly out of line of the direction as shown on the map but is the only crossing. There are more gates here.

The Linn Letch and the Black Burn join to form the Rugley Burn, crossed earlier at the ford. This flows into the Cawledge Burn, which in turn flows into the Aln.

Turn left after crossing and walk upstream beside the straight ditch of the Black Burn. A line of electricity poles indicates the general direction towards the wide metal gate atop the embankment enclosing the disused railway. The gate is a yard or so left of the line of electric wires overhead, and the route crosses the disused railway at a level section between an embankment, left, and a cutting, right. Through the small rough field, past the Half-Crown Well, come out into a vast field and follow the right-hand perimeter to a wicket gate leading to a tree-lined grass track. Follow this for about a quarter-mile to the ruins of High Hobberlaw Farm, almost hidden by trees on the right. Hobberlaw Farm is visible directly down the slope on the right. Intake Farm, passed earlier in the walk, is about a quarter-mile ahead, and this is the point where the longer route joins the much shorter variation.

Leave the Intake track and turn north on an open track to a gate leading into an area of humps and howls, very much overgrown with gorse, hawthorn and tall firs. The track makes a decided loop to the left and back round the central hollow, an old disused quarry. Continue north and downhill in a direct line away from the quarry. Walk to the right of a line of small beech trees and a wicket gate on the left. Through this go down again in the same general direction at the side of the field. A stile lower down leads to the correct side of the fence for the right of way. Walk either side. A gate at the bottom gives access to the corner of the drive down from a long timber building. The drive leads out to the road, the B6341.

Turn right on the road, cross to the pavement on the far side and continue for a short distance to where a lane leads off to the left opposite quarry workings. Follow the lane to the Y-junction and leave the main lane to turn right by the single-storey dwelling along a track between hawthorn and flowering currant. Continue to a T-junction and turn left on the road beside a stone house with a creeper-covered façade. The road descends to Woodbine Cottage and a kissing gate.

Beyond this there are several tracks. Take the centre one towards the lower end of a line of houses and to the right of a playing field. When the path reaches the high wall enclosing Hulne Park, part of Alnwick Castle estate, follow it down to the park gates. Turn right here to return directly to the town centre or cross to the wicket gate and take the riverside path.

Hulne Park is open to the public on Saturdays and Sundays between 1 p.m. and sunset or by arrangement with the estate office.

Notice the monument at the roadside near the park gates commemorating the fact that William the Lion of Scotland, who besieged Alnwick Castle, was taken prisoner in 1174.